D0216366

PRAISE FOR
SPARKING SUCCESS

How can the different creative arts inspire better leadership and management? This wide-ranging book gives insight and, what's more, a helpful guide for practical action.
Rob Goffee, Emeritus Professor of Organizational Behaviour, London Business School

In *Sparking Success*, Adam Kingl nimbly offers a journey of first-hand lessons from leaders in the arts on how to unlock our own creativity to be natural and genuinely effective at whatever it is that we do.
Dina Dommett, Dean of Ashridge, Hult International Business School

A wonderful book that explores how ideas and practices from the arts world – including theatre, television, music, writing and painting – can help us enhance creativity at both the individual and the organizational level. This is a powerful book, full of ideas, practical tools and inspiring stories to guide us on the journey to developing a creative mindset. It belongs on the shelf of every leader!
Costas Markides, Professor of Strategy and Robert P Bauman Chair in Strategic Leadership, London Business School

Sparking Success achieves exactly what the title promises: it helps leaders become more creative, an essential attribute in our unfamiliar times of opportunity, challenge and change. Adam Kingl is a masterful writer about business and leadership – insightful, engaging and highly original.

Jeremy Kourdi, writer, entrepreneur and former Senior Vice President of *The Economist*

Adam Kingl bridges the gap between creative idea generation and practical business application. Highly recommended!

Michael J Gelb, author, executive coach and management consultant

Adam Kingl has roamed the realms of jazz, cooking, writing and the performing arts in search of nuggets of wisdom for hard-pressed leaders who urgently need to innovate. He has returned with a treasure trove of practical ideas on how to weave creativity into your life and work.

Greg Orme, keynote speaker, author and facilitator

Adam Kingl tackles one of the greatest challenges that organizations face – how to improve creativity, innovation and adaptability – by applying lessons from some of the most innovative leaders on the planet. This book is inspiring, warm-hearted and highly applicable.

Sharmla Chetty, CEO, Duke Corporate Education, Duke University

Adam Kingl's new book is truly inspiring, drawing on threads from history, neuroscience, jazz, improvisation, storytelling and art to weave together a colourfully vivid tapestry representing human adaptation and innovation, and describe how organizations can impactfully and positively contribute to improving the world through novel, cutting-edge thinking and practices.

John Davis, Professor of Practice, Lundquist College of Business, University of Oregon

Adam Kingl is inspirational, comprehensive and practical and provides rich context to a critical 21st-century question: how to bring creativity to work? If you are interested in restoring creativity or leading creatives, read this book!

David Brown, Director of Executive Education, Imperial College Business School

Written by an author steeped in highly creative cultures, as well as top-notch learning environments, *Sparking Success* is a brilliantly written, practical guide that will unlock your and your team's creativity.

Richard Hytner, former Worldwide Deputy Chairman of Saatchi & Saatchi and Adjunct Professor of Marketing at London Business School

Through his global work in executive education, Adam Kingl has extensive real-world experience working with senior executives and leaders from a diverse group of industries and sectors. This sets him firmly apart from so many others in this space, and he brings it all to bear here in a book harnessing a kaleidoscope of viewpoints to unleash the power of creativity for true business impact.

Bruce Wiesner, Associate Dean, Executive Education, UBC Sauder School of Business

Sparking Success

Why every leader needs to
develop a creative mindset

Adam Kingl

KoganPage

First published in Great Britain and the United States in 2023 by Kogan Page

2nd Floor, 45 Gee Street
London
EC1V 3RS
United Kingdom
www.koganpage.com

8 W 38th Street, Suite 902
New York, NY 10018
USA

4737/23 Ansari Road
Daryaganj
New Delhi 110002
India

© Adam Kingl, 2023

The right of Adam Kingl to be identified as the author of this work has been asserted by him in accordance with the Copyright, Designs and Patents Act 1988.

ISBNs
Hardback   978 1 3986 0960 0
Paperback   978 1 3986 0958 7
Ebook   978 1 3986 0959 4

British Library Cataloguing-in-Publication Data
A CIP record for this book is available from the British Library.

Library of Congress Cataloging-in-Publication Data
Names: Kingl, Adam, author.
Title: Sparking success: why every leader needs to develop a creative mindset / Adam Kingl.
Description: 1st Edition. | New York, NY: Kogan Page Inc, [2023] | Includes bibliographical references and index.
Identifiers: LCCN 2022058569 (print) | LCCN 2022058570 (ebook) | ISBN 9781398609587 (paperback) | ISBN 9781398609600 (hardback) | ISBN 9781398609594 (ebook)
Subjects: LCSH: Creative ability in business. | Organizational change. | Leadership.
Classification: LCC HD53 .K5646 2023 (print) | LCC HD53 (ebook) | DDC 650.1–dc23/eng/20221208
LC record available at https://lccn.loc.gov/2022058569
LC ebook record available at https://lccn.loc.gov/2022058570

Typeset by Hong Kong FIVE Workshop, Hong Kong
Print production managed by Jellyfish
Printed and bound by CPI Group (UK) Ltd, Croydon CR0 4YY

*This work is dedicated to all those
who teach the creative arts. You nourish the soul,
make meaning out of the void and remind us
what it is to be human.*

'The lucky few who can be involved in
creative work of any sort will be
the true elite of humankind, for they alone will
do more than serve a machine.'
Isaac Asimov

'What do you do, Daddy?'
'I help people to be creative.'
'Is that because they've forgotten?'
**Giles Ford in conversation with
his seven-year-old son Arthur**

CONTENTS

01
A new Renaissance

The case for bringing creative and corporate closer together

Every human being on the planet possesses an abundance of creativity, adaptability and inspiration, and it stands to reason that when we come together in these communities that we call companies there should be a multiplier effect. Yet our collective effort usually only produces a deficit of these characteristics. Our organizations typically suffer from little to no creativity. In fact, focus on innovation in recent years has been cut in half according to a McKinsey study of more than 200 global companies.[1] I doubt that claim shocked you; we intuitively know this to be true. Why is this so? Primarily, we are burdened by underlying assumptions of how we are supposed to organize work, assumptions that for the most part originated at least 150 years ago at the dawn of the Industrial Revolution. We can uncover better solutions to fill the deep craters in our corporate spirit with the creative, fluid and humanistic approaches from artists and innovators as well, rather than solely from management engineers.

At the same time, agility – the ability to pivot, invent and reinvent – has never been more important in a world where change itself is occurring at a scale and pace that can leave us breathless. Our ability to keep up is a key leadership capability today. Of course, one industry has always been creative and ever evolving, and that's the arts. Might we be able to apply its leadership lessons to any other industry in order to unlock further human capability? I believe we can.

My belief derives from a professional lifetime advising corporations on their creative leadership, which in turn has been informed by my professional background in theatre, business and academia. I have a master's in both business administration and in fine arts, have worked in the creative and administrative functions of arts organizations, have backed up my lifetime's work with research and writing as a faculty member in world-class universities, and have taught and consulted to corporations in dozens of industries and countries on nurturing their creativity, adaptability and human-centricity. Now I want to pass on my tools, evidence and stories so you can start or continue the journey yourself.

Our approach

To do this, the next chapter will, perhaps counterintuitively, uncover some of the science of creativity. Recent neuroscientific research explains the obstacles that our brains put between ourselves and inspiration. This useful context underpins the rest of the book. Then, the core chapters three to eight all share the same structure. I will set out problems or obstacles to innovation and adaptability, then observe how one artistic medium explodes those obstacles. In exploring those creative media, I've interviewed prominent leaders from theatre, television, music, writing, cooking and painting, and uncover their approaches to keep themselves and their teams refreshed in their ability and enthusiasm to adapt, create and learn. These core chapters also tell the stories of companies in more traditional industries and how they have applied the same or similar approaches, demonstrating that creative and adaptive habits are not found solely in the realm of artistic organizations. Each chapter concludes with 'One thing you can do on Monday morning', a detailed, practical exercise or technique that you can practise in order to enhance your own or your team's creative and adaptive capacity. In this manner, *Sparking Success* is not merely a concept book but one that offers strategies and tactics for the busy professional to apply impactful techniques right away.

This book derives lessons from the arts and imports them into all those areas of business where the industrial age has not and will not provide the full solutions – how we lead and manage teams, ideate, innovate, adapt, plan and organize. In so doing, rather than finding answers in the discipline of scientific management as perfected by Henry Ford and Frederick Winslow Taylor, we will look to Renaissance thinking. Our dialogue will integrate artistic and technological insights from modern-day creative leaders who are continuing the legacies of Leonardo da Vinci and Lorenzo de' Medici, when the Medici patronage of Florentine art and science coalesced in brilliant invention that integrated philosophy, anatomy, engineering and aesthetic. As a result of this interchange between commerce and the arts, among many benefits Florentines witnessed the emergence of the modern banking system developing 'in parallel with the most important artistic flowering in the history of the western world'.[2]

But one of the most pernicious of our obstacles to usher in a new Renaissance is what we understand to be the very purpose of management. Look in any thesaurus in almost any language on the planet and the first synonym you'll find for the verb 'to manage' is 'to control'.[3] Our philosophy of management is predicated on absolute control, driving efficiency in and variance out. I'm not saying we don't require some degree of control in our companies – if we had no control, we'd have chaos! But can we say that there is *any balance whatsoever* between control on one side of the spectrum and innovation, agency and adaptability on the other?

So what is the *right* balance? If we give our people one hour a week to create or collaborate to solve our most intractable problems, is that sufficient to drive innovation into the warp and weft of our corporate fabric? I hope you'd agree that it is not. The question is: if our people had, say, 20 per cent of their time to explore great ideas and talk to customers outside the office walls, brainstorm new solutions to problems they haven't managed to solve for years, identify new ways of working that would be more exciting and inspirational, what would be the impact on our organizational life? How would the concept of 'work' change? What would be our new dominant image when we hear that word 'work'?

At every conference at which I speak, with every corporate client with whom I consult, I hear that we need to achieve a greater balance between the art and the science of work, particularly when the conversation turns to innovation. But we feel stuck, unable to make the changes we know we must. A Boston Consulting Group study asked CEOs where innovation ranked as a strategic priority.[4]

Seventy-nine per cent said it was a top three priority, and you have to wonder why that number wasn't 100 per cent since you could argue that innovation is the only protection for remaining relevant. So innovation is not *an* advantage, it is *the* advantage! However, a McKinsey study reported that 94 per cent of employees say their organization is ineffective at innovation.[5] I'm not sure that there is a bigger gap in our companies between how critical CEOs think something is and how bad we are at it, between what we know we *need* to do and what we *actually* do.

A significant factor behind this knowing–doing gap is that since the beginning of the Industrial Age we've been trained as leaders to push out those very human qualities that would better enable our organizations to navigate these turbulent waters: inspiration, innovation, adaptability, empowerment, curiosity. While business has worked very hard to drive out these qualities, with its incessant preference to value only those merits which can be acutely measured, the arts have always toiled to drive them in.

Yet the reason I am optimistic today is that we happen to live during one of those inflection points of history. Scientific management has had its day in the sun, making many executives and investors admittedly very wealthy. We now require a new Renaissance, a flowering of interchange between the arts and business whereby we recreate work around human fulfilment. In the privileged position of a consultant and educator to executives, I hear from leaders all around the world who are feeling an unprecedented pressure to reinvent how they lead, learn, operate, structure, incentivize, hire, promote and communicate. Business must reflect the needs of its employees, customers and society in better ways than those we have experienced. If the leadership of the corporate estate requires reimagining, then the new solutions will come less from the *science* of management and more from the *art*.

If you're creative and you know it, raise your hand

If we're going to adopt more practices from the arts in order to be fit for tomorrow, we might well ask if we have sufficiently innate creativity to accomplish this goal. In facilitating workshops on innovation for business, I usually begin the sessions by asking, 'Please raise your hand if you do *not* regularly think of yourself as a creative person.' Almost inevitably, I'm confronted with a forest of arms signalling agreement with this statement. But if we reflect on our childhoods, we intuitively understand that the exact opposite would be true. As children, we are supremely creative human beings.

The late Professor George Land at the University of Minnesota assessed 1,600 people in their development from children to adults on their 'genius' levels of creativity, defined as 'divergent thinking'. Research had already established that high IQ and creative aptitude are not correlated. At ages 3 to 5, 98 per cent of the test subjects scored as creative geniuses. At ages 8 to 10, that percentage plummeted to 32 per cent. At ages 13 to 15, only 10 per cent were geniuses, and by age 25 a paltry 2 per cent were still creative paragons. Notice that by the time these children reached adulthood, their creative capacity had completely and exactly *inverted*.[6] At the youngest ages, only 2 per cent were not creative geniuses, and as adults only 2 per cent still were geniuses.

These results may not surprise us. When I discuss this study, most people respond that school and society are to blame, incentivizing conformity and 'one right answer' thinking. If that diagnosis is true, then the solution is apparent as well. For us individually as adults and collectively as organizations, we must rediscover at least some of the rhythms, routines, incentives and habits that we practised as children. For starters, I'm sure we all remember that a typical day as small children included an abundance of art and play. Isn't it funny that the corporations that we celebrate today, from Google to Kickstarter to Pixar to LEGO, create those same environments of art and play in their cultures that most of our organizations work terribly hard to suppress?

While I am indeed advocating for revolutionizing how we work, I stress that such revolutions begin at the level of the individual within their own work life. Leaders of course have an overweighted influence over what is prioritized and how their culture is role modelled among their teams and organizations. The payoff then has a high rate of return in that a small degree of personal change may catalyze widespread shifts in habit and mindset in the people around the leader. Such shifts then allow both leader and team, and even company, to actually enable the priorities of innovation, adaptability and inspiration to materialize rather than eternally languish as aspirations.

Perhaps my ambition that you might revolutionize your approach to work daunts you: 'Revolutionize is a pretty strong word, Adam. I'm no revolutionary!' Well, history teaches us a very useful lesson about successful revolutions. First, they are not always about violently overthrowing regimes. We can observe technological, social or philosophical revolutions too. In most cases, these revolutions started simply by questioning an assumption and finding ways to try doing something a little differently. Let's see if there's hope for us today to achieve dramatic reinvention by examining our past.

A short history of revolutionary innovation

If we think back, way back, throughout human history, we can identify revolutions of philosophy, social organization or technology where society was vastly enriched as a consequence. At the moment of the introduction of each discovery, life was dramatically different from before. With that vital improvement came a transformation in society and culture. You only have to think about the advent of the internet and the smartphone to consider recent examples. Peering into our distant past, survival was made easier by a tool such as the wheel or a process such as agriculture. In either case, an assumption or mindset was overthrown which made those revolutions possible.

In order to understand what we require for the next revolution in our world of work, and what assumptions we may need to overthrow to get there, it's useful to explore the explosion of some of these long-held mindsets. I will not investigate every period of human evolution (I'm sure you're silently thanking me for that!), but I believe that history can teach us as much about our present condition as it does about our past.

Nomadic to settled

If we peer as far back as we can go in human history, the Mesolithic period (about 13000–8000 BCE but harder to be precise when we're prehistoric) witnessed a revolution from tribes hunting large animals as the primary form of sustenance to a more hunter-gatherer way of life. This change meant that groups shifted from a nomadic lifestyle to a more settled one. Tools became more sophisticated, from crude, heavy weaponry to pottery and knives. Humans had more time to create and imagine when they weren't always on the move. For the same reason, as communities settled we begin to see the early expression of art. The overthrown assumption in this epoch was that tribes had to be nomadic in order to survive.

Hunter-gatherer to farmer

The Neolithic period (8000–4500 BCE) witnessed the introduction of agriculture. Humans learned how plants could be cultivated and which ones were easier to grow. For farming to be possible, societies created life-changing routines such as irrigation, animal domestication and trade. The overthrown assumption was that the land's yield was only down to nature rather than to human cultivation as well.

Settlements to empires

In the Bronze Age (3300–1200 BCE), after learning to leverage plants and animals towards their aims, people manipulated minerals with ever greater sophistication. Stronger materials led to new and better dwellings and other buildings.

As knowledge disseminated at a new scale through writing, society benefited materially with the growth of cities, creatively with an explosion of art and architecture, and socially with the emergence of empires such as Egypt and Mesopotamia. The assumptions that fell in this period were that knowledge transmission was only verbal and pictorial, and that there were limits to the potential size of human settlements.

Survival to civilization

Because of the ever-growing size and sophistication of cities, humans then turned their thoughts to what it really means to live, co-exist and learn. In Classical Greece (500–323 BCE), much of the West's baselines of political, philosophical and artistic thought were articulated. Old assumptions of social organization revolving around servitude and survival made way for a new era centred around the concept and philosophy of civilization itself and a proactive wrestling with metaphysical questions as a critical component of the human experience.

The Roman Empire as the spiritual heir of ancient Greece applied a new rigour to how we organize effort. The Roman military structured itself in a hierarchical manner, with legions composed of ranked officers (an early managerial class) in an organizational design that looks remarkably familiar today in any medium- to large-scale human architecture, be it in the military, corporate or public sector. Ask just about any company on the planet to show you a chart of how they're organized, and the shape you are most likely to see is a pyramid. We have the Romans to thank for that.

Exclusive to integrated

Fast forward to the Renaissance (1300–1600) and we observe a flowering of art, culture, education and commerce. The assumption that these disciplines were wholly distinct was destroyed in this era. To integrate them was to unlock innovation and create wealth. Lorenzo de' Medici, self-deprecatingly known as Lorenzo the Magnificent, ruled the Florentine city-state and transformed the economy from wool production to modern banking. At the same time, he sponsored the art and science of Leonardo da Vinci, who designed many concepts, including the helicopter *centuries* before we saw it realized. A few years later, Galileo championed heliocentrism, invented the thermometer and revealed Venus' moons, and that is not a euphemism.

Meanwhile, the exploration of the human condition, the layperson's excavation of the soul, occurred just across the English Channel in London by one Mr William Shakespeare, who freshly examined the nature of leadership and what it is to be led by kings who are granted divinity but cannot grasp it. As his Richard II chides, 'You have mistook me all this while. I live with bread like you, feel, want, taste grief, need friends. Subjected thus, how can you say to me I am a king?'[7]

All of these snapshots of this era illustrate that the Renaissance was undoubtedly one of the most profoundly important periods of societal development in human history. Commerce, science and the arts intermingled in a synergy that benefited each estate. In other words, the arts not only benefited from economic prosperity, but artistic endeavour contributed to that abundance.

Human expression to human engineering

In humankind's quest to perfect the process by which we create wealth, the previous ménage à trois among science, business and art became a cosier domestic arrangement between science and commerce, elbowing the arts into the periphery in terms of the habits, goals and philosophies of leadership and organizational life. This paucity of artistic creativity and inspiration was a symptom of the Industrial Revolution (1760–1914), which perfected the philosophy of Frederick Winslow Taylor's scientific management, whose hypothesis was that the way in which we organize business is to drive efficiency in and variance out, implying a human labourer is but a cog in an industrial machine. Taylorism was specifically perfect for the manufacturing heyday of a century ago when Henry Ford once famously quipped, 'Why is it every time I hire a pair of hands, a brain comes attached?'[8] Over a short period of time, the skyscape of business lost its constellation of artistic exploration – a critical mindset laid to waste. We dehumanized our companies in perfecting Taylorism and combined that philosophy with the obeyance-driven, hierarchical architecture of the Roman legions. Yet today, we lament that we lack humanity in our work life. Why are we surprised?

How bad is it?

How bad and how widespread is the problem? We can quantify it. The polling company Gallup has conducted a massive survey of hundreds of thousands of employees in 142 countries every other year, asking about their engagement at work. In the last survey as of this writing, a paltry 13 per cent reported that they were 'engaged', in other words emotionally invested in their work. Sixty-three per cent answered that they were 'not engaged', or emotionally disconnected and less likely to be productive. An alarming 24 per cent responded that they were 'actively disengaged', meaning they essentially hated their work or would even commit sabotage given half a chance.[9] Now, some of us are moved by numbers, some by words and others by images. Allow me to illustrate how alarming this global situation is with a simple picture. Let's say you're an average company with 100 employees. If you lined them up in a room, you'd see this:

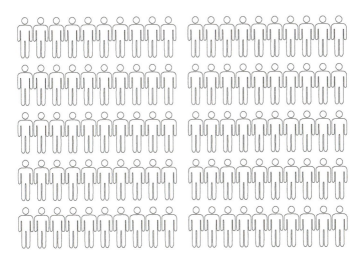

Now let's pretend that you, as this company's leader, asked everyone who is 'engaged at work' to paint themselves grey. Don't worry, it's a hypothetical exercise. This is what you'd see now:

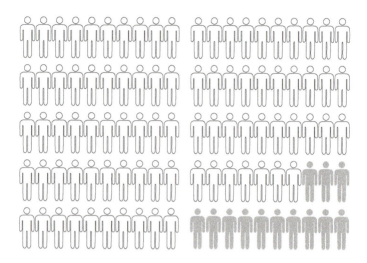

What is the emotion you'd feel in the pit of your gut looking out over such a room full of colleagues and seeing how few are with and for you? For me, visualizing 'only 13 per cent engaged at work' colours me with a whole new patina of despair, guilt and urgency. Now consider the 200 million companies in the world, some with thousands or even millions[10] of employees, and this image is truly frightening! The vast majority of the planet's workforce is emotionally detached, if not royally pissed off. It's at least a sign that revolution is in the air.

The fault does not reside with our front-line employees but with our leaders and their philosophy of governance from an era and context that effectively ended half a century ago. Some predicted that the digital revolution or information age was to herald a nirvana of wealth and contentment. But while the technologies and industries changed, the manner in which we organized work did not, so work-life continues to be unlivable. The German sociologist Max Weber remarked, 'The fate of our times is characterized by rationalization and intellectualization and, above all, by the disenchantment of the world.'[11] We still find ourselves in a cage of our own making, unprepared for a world in which the need for humanizing is increasing by the hour.

The time is now

Returning to our journey through history, you may have noticed that the epochs of civilization that we outlined compressed from years measured in thousands to hundreds to just decades. In other words, we have less time in every epoch to prepare for the next revolution. The below helps to visualize the dramatically squeezed amount of time that we have to pivot from one era to the next.

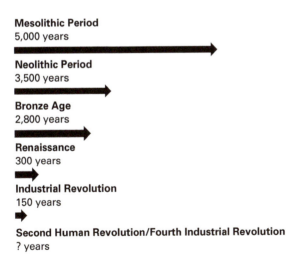

Mesolithic Period
5,000 years

Neolithic Period
3,500 years

Bronze Age
2,800 years

Renaissance
300 years

Industrial Revolution
150 years

Second Human Revolution/Fourth Industrial Revolution
? years

Therefore, adaptability, creativity and inspiration are *the* leadership qualities that our organizations require today. Both employer and employee need these capabilities now, and we don't have centuries to develop them anymore. Making these qualities preeminent in our organizations is the next revolution. You can be at the forefront of this changing tide, and this book will help take you there.

In rediscovering art and play, two virtuous habits that spark and nurture those characteristics of innovation including divergent thinking, collaboration, mindfulness, inspiration, exploring untraditional ideas and picturing the future, we uncover anew the state of mind and spirit that we have always naturally possessed. We begin to encourage an environment that allows our companies collectively to discover what we know individually that we have always craved.

Endnotes

1 Jordan Bar Am, Laura Furstenthal, Felicitas Jorge and Erik Roth, 'Innovation in a crisis: Why it is more critical than ever', McKinsey, 17 June 2020, https://www.mckinsey.com/business-functions/strategy-and-corporate-finance/our-insights/innovation-in-a-crisis-why-it-is-more-critical-than-ever (archived at https://perma.cc/2B5C-VR9X)

2 Jonathan Jones, 'The Medicis: Money, myth and mystery', *The Guardian*, 10 August 2011.

3 Thank you to Prof. Gary Hamel of London Business School for identifying this.

4 Michael Ringel, Andrew Taylor and Hadi Zablit, 'The most innovative companies 2015', BCG Report, 2 December 2015.

5   Paul Cobban, Rahul Nair and Natalie Painchaud, 'Breaking down the barriers to innovation', *Harvard Business Review*, November–December 2019.

6   Greg Orme, *The Human Edge* (Harlow: Pearson Education, 2019), 48–49.

7   William Shakespeare, *Richard II*, in *The Riverside Shakespeare*, ed. G Blakemore Evans (Boston: Houghton Mifflin, 1974), III, ii, 174–77.

8   Bob Clinkert, 'What Henry Ford really thinks of you', 25 October 2013, https://blog.unleashthemasterpiece.com/ what-henry-ford-really-thinks-of-you-full-article/ (archived at https://perma.cc/W9XE-J3BT)

9   Gallup, 'State of the global workplace', https://www.gallup.de/ 183833/state-the-global-workplace.aspx (archived at https://perma.cc/P2BS-UXNT)

10 There are quite a few multi-million-person organizations in the world, including the US Department of Defense, Walmart, McDonald's and the UK National Health Service.

11 Anthony Cascardi, *The Subject of Modernity* (Cambridge: Cambridge University Press, 1992).

02

How are we creative?

The realm of neuroscience

Is creativity a product of nature or nurture? While some people have a higher proclivity to creative expression, we all have the potential; it's part of human nature. But we are forced to specialize so early in our development that we shut down pursuits, interests and disciplines unconscionably early. The arts are often the first to go, either because parents push their children towards so-called 'safe' subjects to set them up for stable careers, such as engineering, mathematics and the like, or schools shove art, music, creative writing and drama into the periphery of the curriculum, if they appear at all. In primary school, I recall that my music and art classes occurred only once a week versus daily sessions in maths, history and science. There may be exceptions, but most schools do not hesitate to shave funding from the arts at the first sign of budget cuts. As the harried principal shouts when firing the titular music teacher in the film *Mr Holland's Opus*, 'If I'm forced to choose between Mozart and reading, writing and long division, I choose long division.' To which, the music teacher, Mr Holland, retorts, 'Well, I guess you can cut the arts as much as you want, Gene. Sooner or later, these kids aren't going to have anything to read or write about.'[1]

Too many schools minimize or ignore creativity, too many parents discourage it and too many companies devalue it. Our firms abrogate responsibility for innovation to a select fraction of the employee population, often someone with a lofty title like Chief Creative Officer, which of course tacitly communicates to the rest of the company that they should leave creativity to the specialists. This is not only a shame but a great waste since 75 per cent of productivity gains can be traced back to bottom-up ideas from front-line employees.[2] Or our company's leaders encourage innovation in their words but deprioritize it in their actions, always selecting the safe, the incremental and the staid in their decisions. Or if we observe how our leaders spend their time, and by extension how we should spend ours, they are tacitly telling us that creativity is relegated to possibly a few minutes a week and ideally in one's free time, not when we're 'on the clock'. In my advisory work, I usually find this last condition, lack of time, to be the most common and pernicious reason why people tell me they cannot be creative at work.

The problem is that if we budget very little time in our lives for innovating or adapting to try new ideas, we typically incur a double deficit in our creative capacity. First, we never make the time because creativity is always at the bottom of our priority list. Inevitably, we can never plan on all the fire-fighting and pop-up meetings that will occur in the week, so our real week is much more full of 'dealing with the day to day' than our diaries suggested on Monday morning.

Second, if we do keep and honour a tiny fraction of our week or month for creative thinking, brainstorming and the like, we find we are constantly distracted, and we never seem to produce anything worthwhile as a result. So we face each new window of opportunity for innovation with an ever-growing, soul-sucking impression of dread or, at the least, resignation.

Neuroscience and the brain

What we're learning now is that we're actually training our brains to deliver this depressing result. Neuroscientific research has revealed how the brain can either repress or invigorate creativity.[3] These hurried, captured moments of precious time for innovation yield paltry results because our brains just can't turn on the magic for such short, unsustainable periods of time.

There are several brain states, from deep sleep to deep focus and peak performance. The higher the performing brain, the greater the frequency of brain waves, hence Hertz is the degree of measurement:

- Delta – deep sleep: 1–3 Hz
- Theta – deep meditation, light sleep: 4–8 Hz
- Alpha – relaxed, calm consciousness: 9–12 Hz
- Beta – normal, alert consciousness: 13–30 Hz
- Gamma – super-focused mind, increased brain power, peak state of consciousness and performance: 31–70 Hz[4]

Which of these do you think is our typical brain state during a normal workday? Beta is probably our usual state, right? This is what we require of our brains to accomplish our normal tasks of answering emails, solving our workaday problems… and possibly Theta state when we're in long committee meetings. Typical business routines encourage us to work in a state where the Beta waves (business as usual) in our brains are dominant, though we now know that maximum innovation and insight occur when we are in Gamma state.

Neuroscientific research has also revealed that our brains can stay in Beta for a long time and that we are in fact conditioned to stay there.[5] As a result, if we crank the mental engine to get up to Gamma, the brain through habit easily and proactively drags us back to Beta. Therefore, if we need our brains to be in Gamma in order to be truly creative, genuinely adding previously unheard-of insight and exponentially big ideas, our brains would struggle to do that in, say, a one-hour meeting once a week, no doubt in the Creative Committee meeting! Beta state is like a constant and familiar noise; it's the ever-present static of our work lives that can block Gamma state. I liken this to how I find it hard to think when I'm eating an apple because I have this magnified, constant crunching noise in the echo chamber of my skull.

Let me illuminate this exact point with a simple experiment that you can easily do wherever you are. I'm going to present you with a classic creative assessment question. This is like your boss giving you a creative challenge in a 45-minute weekly meeting (but it's never actually 45 minutes long, is it, because Carl always comes late. We all have a Carl, don't we?).

You just need a piece of paper, a writing utensil, and a stopwatch or phone programmed to beep after 30 seconds. And you need something crunchy to eat: celery, apple… you get the picture. Please stop reading here if you're going to do the exercise and collect these items now. Don't worry, I'll wait.

Welcome back. Once you read the question in the next paragraph, start the 30-second clock and write down a list of as many answers as you possibly can before the time expires. You're going for quantity, not quality. Here we go:

What are all the possible uses of a paper clip?

How did you do? I'm sure you had many more answers to list but you ran out of time. Don't fret. Now you get to continue your list… with a twist. Reset your stopwatch for 30 seconds and repeat the exercise but eat the crunchy thing while you're making your list. OK – go for it!

Welcome back. I bet the exercise was much harder the second time. In addition to the probability that you wrote many of the obvious answers during the first attempt, you just created a metaphor for the creative mind in the workplace. We represented the interference in your brain imposed by all the tasks and challenges in the work week, the Beta wave activity demanding your time, with the crunching noise in your head.

We can't easily shut off this Beta activity, the laundry list of actions and decisions we have to make, even if we're completely confident in our ability to make them. Beta is our habit, our rhythm, our tyranny. Because we don't have balance between the mundane and the creative, returning to the Renaissance theme of balance and integration, we can't achieve creativity even if we give ourselves those fleeting 30 minutes a week to do so. We must change our routines so that we give our brains more time to marinate in Gamma and increase the frequency of those marinades. Like any muscle, the creative function in our brain requires exercise in order to improve, but as importantly, to be receptive to create in the first place.

The point is not that we denude all traditional routine from our organizations – we need some of that. But the hundreds of companies that I've worked with usually operate at a ratio of about 99 per cent business as usual to 1 per cent creative time... in a good week! So if you're feeling uncomfortable that I might be suggesting something like a 50–50 balance, I'm not necessarily saying that. But the better ratio surely has to be closer to 80–20 at least? I'm merely entreating us to ask ourselves honestly, 'Is the balance right?'

Google and 3M have famously offered '20 per cent time' for some of their employees, giving them complete freedom to use that 20 per cent, one day a week, to pursue their own passion projects. These are very successful companies, yet when I discuss 20 per cent time with others, the first pushback I almost always hear is, 'Yeah, but some people are just going to use their free time to go golfing.' My response: 'So what?' There are at least two reasons for my provocative answer.

First, we have to trust that the majority of our colleagues will responsibly pursue the freedom that we return to their lives for inspiration and passion. One also has to ask why you would hire these people in the first place if you don't even trust them enough to use their work time conscientiously?

Second, for Google, that 20 per cent time ultimately yielded products like Gmail and Google Maps. If I can get that kind of return on investment, I don't really care if a tiny fraction squanders that time. Management in the 21st century, in a new Renaissance, will have to be focused on making our companies more about encouraging relevance for tomorrow, *sparking success* with inspiration, and less about building in even more control.

The majority of this book is about identifying the lessons we can learn from the routines, habits and mindsets that one would typically practise in the creative arts and then applying those to traditional industry practices, just as we've seen with Google and 3M, in order to enhance our innovation, agility and engagement. But science, and particularly neuroscience, certainly have a role to play in this dialogue as well. If we're going to reshape our companies, then it can't hurt to understand how we're wired, how and why our brains resist or accelerate their capacity to adapt. Now that we understand some of the chemistry of creativity and adaptation, we can get on with how to be the catalyst in the coming chapters.

One thing you can do on Monday morning

I attempt to stay firmly and proudly in the practitioner camp in terms of my perspective and professional life. Research is a tremendous gift to humankind in our search for truth, particularly in this age of so-called 'fake news'. Could I say anything less, given I've spent most of my life studying in and working for universities? But for the realm in which I operate in terms of my clients, that of the business world, the most important question to answer is, 'What do I *do* with this insight? How does this move me or my organization forward?' So, I will conclude the following chapters with suggestions for how you can apply some of the insights. In this way, the book resembles an executive education programme in miniature, a dialogue that is ultimately action-focused rather than hypothetical musing.

For this chapter's suggested actions, we know that we have to build in time for the brain to focus on the new and unexpected, proactively seeking surprise, reflection and experimentation. The best advice an executive coach ever gave me was to block out time, at least three hours but ideally a day, in my diary every week just for me. This time was sacrosanct; no one could get a meeting or call with me during that window unless the topic was specifically a creative or adaptive challenge. And this coach was adamant that I should not use the time to catch up with work. It was not 'free' time but had its own purpose, which was most certainly not to fulfil the day to day but to engage my creative muscles.

I found that Friday afternoons worked best for a couple of reasons. First, as the work week was nearing its close, colleagues and clients slowed their pace a little and some escaped early for the weekend, so it was easier to keep that time blocked out. Second, since changing my environment would also stimulate different neurons in my brain, Friday afternoons were also easier to spend outside my or my clients' offices. Surely maximizing my creative opportunities would not be best served sitting at my desk at work, staring at my trusty laptop, waiting for inspiration to pounce, jaguar-like, onto my unsuspecting scalp. So even if I did book a creative meeting with a colleague, I would usually insist that we hold it elsewhere: a park, museum, gallery, funky café, you get the idea. This tip reminds me of a similar piece of advice given to me by one of my mentors many years ago: 'Pick different routes to work.' In other words, don't get stuck in routine, and allow yourself to be surprised by different sights, paths, parks, trains, bus routes, stores, blocks and people.

The funny thing is that when I did have a meeting outside the office in an untraditional space, inevitably my colleagues would comment how refreshing and stimulating it was to meet in a new environment, yet when the next meeting request came along, they usually suggested meeting at our desks or in a bland conference room again! It just goes to show how pernicious and deep our habits are, how dominant and comforting it is to dwell in Beta state. It would be comforting to assume we could disrupt our environments and routines as little as possible and somehow transform into creative geniuses through willpower alone. As Hemingway mused in *The Sun Also Rises*, 'Isn't it pretty to think so?'[6] But our own brains' habits oppose that ambition until we train them to be receptive.

Endnotes

1 *Mr Holland's Opus*, directed by Stephen Herek (Burbank, CA: Hollywood Pictures, 1995).

2 Bilal Gokpinar, 'Driving efficiency gains starts with frontline employee innovation', UCL School of Management, 21 July 2021, https://www.mgmt.ucl.ac.uk/news/driving-efficiency-gains-starts-frontline-employee-innovation (archived at https://perma.cc/F5YM-7DZ7)

3 Estanislao Bachrach, *The Agile Mind* (London: Virgin Books, 2012).

4 Neurohealth, https://nhahealth.com/brainwaves-the-language/ (archived at https://perma.cc/KLC7-7YWW)

5 Christopher Bergland, 'Alpha brain waves boost creativity and reduce depression', *Psychology Today*, 17 April 2015; Mark Travers, 'Feeling uninspired? Here's what new science says about breaking through a creative block', *Forbes*, 2 September 2022; Kelton Reid, 'How to overcome writer's block with neuroscience', 19 May 2022, https://copyblogger.com/overcome-writers-block/ (archived at https://perma.cc/2S62-US69)

6 Ernest Hemingway, *The Sun Also Rises* (London: Arrow Classic, New Ed., 1994).

03
Nurturing spontaneity

The realm of jazz and improvisation

How do we prevent teams from growing stale in the number, novelty and quality of new ideas? First, leaders typically struggle to add room for adaptability, a fun and productive ideation dynamic, and quick evolution and iteration of ideas. Second, leaders must do a better job of building in exercises, habits and systems that encourage innovation and horizon-stretching. What are the processes and norms of those individuals that are dedicated to making creative pursuit a habit?

We'll reveal new insights from jazz pianist and ensemble leader Alex Steele, who also delivers workshops applying jazz and its lessons to corporate audiences. Steele uses music to get people to overcome the belief that because they are not an expert, they should not contribute. He has asked bankers who have never played an instrument before to play the keyboard with his jazz group in order to help them gain the confidence to make suggestions, observe, listen and respond to their environment. We also speak to improvisational theatre pioneer Neil Mullarkey, who founded London's Comedy Store Players with film star Mike Myers. We will explicitly show how you can apply their improvisation principles to your work environment.

Jazz

Alex Steele grew up in a family of professional musicians: both parents, his grandfather, and many uncles, aunts and cousins. He learned music informally through immersion and he calls music his first language, even before English. In his early twenties, Steele was a session musician, a film composer and a music teacher. After a year backpacking across Europe, the Middle East and Asia, he studied environmental sciences at university. In his early career, he worked by day as a consultant, educator and academic, while by night he moonlighted performing on the piano at jazz clubs. Studying and consulting on climate change, Steele was struck by how clear the solutions are but how difficult it is to change human behaviour to implement those solutions. Turning his attention to this challenge, Steele considered if and how his experience with jazz could illuminate the conditions that relax the rigidity of our behaviours, assumptions and habits.

Fifteen years ago, Steele asked a mentor at Ashridge-Hult International Business School in Hertfordshire, UK for his advice. They agreed that Steele should experiment with delivering a jazz workshop as a way of considering how to unlock change as part of an Ashridge corporate executive education programme. It was so successful that more programme directors asked Steele to deliver this session for them, until he left his job at the University of Gloucestershire to design and deliver these workshops full time. Incidentally, and not insignificantly, Steele reflects that he now plays jazz professionally more than he ever has – by day as part of his engagements with corporate audiences and at night at jazz clubs and festivals all over the world.

A jazz musician will often tour alone and perform with local pick-up bands. They have to be comfortable with 'not knowing'. In Steele's experience, when a jazz ensemble meets for the first time, they do not need to have made a plan or to rehearse. They get to know one another in real time as they begin their performance in front of the audience, and all they need to start is a known melody or a harmonic framework (the chords) from which to begin. This provides the canvas upon which they can improvise. In this way and in its evolving traditions, jazz has a structure and a vocabulary. Once you have that, you can play anywhere and do not require a consistent leader. Unlike a conversation, where there's chaos if more than one person is talking at the same time, a jazz band can swap who is leading but its followers are never silent. 'We tell a story but we don't know in advance what it will be,' says Steele. 'It's based on our mood, dynamic and connection with the audience.'[1]

Letting go of expertise

Jazz is composition and performance occurring at the same time. It's finding beauty and value in combining notes. It's the beginner's mind, letting go of expertise and starting with a blank canvas each time. As Shunryu Suzuki, who helped popularize Zen Buddhism in the United States, describes, 'In the beginner's mind there are many possibilities, but in the expert's there are few.'[2] Organizations need to be more willing to experiment with such non-hierarchical, non-expert models, like the company W L Gore, whose employees have no titles. At Gore, you know you're a leader if you call a meeting and people come. It requires humility for a leader to let go of positional authority as some kind of proxy for expertise. After the fear, there's a joy in letting go and knowing that your colleagues want to contribute and help you succeed.

Jazz pianist Keith Jarrett experienced a sublime example of surrendering any expectation of perfection, and allowing oneself to be surprised, when he played at the Cologne Opera House in 1975. Jarrett was always particular about the type of piano he expected at each venue to which he travelled, how the instrument was positioned on stage, and so on. You can imagine his consternation, then, when he discovered that the piano in Cologne was small, out of tune, several keys didn't work at all(!), and the instrument possessed a dodgy sustain pedal. His first instinct was to call for a new piano, but none was available. His second instinct was to call off the concert, but ECM Records founder and producer Manfred Eicher convinced him to just give it a go. Jarrett recalled, 'I have to do this. I'm doing it. I don't care what the f*** the piano sounds like. I'm doing it!'[3] The concert became legendary because Jarret, in the words of Steele, 'played with what he had'. He moved away from some parts of the piano where the tone was poor, changed his normal posture because of the piano's small size and low volume, simply avoided the keys which didn't work, and just let go. As a result, he played in a way he never had before and undeliberately created a masterpiece. Luckily for the world, though Jarrett had instructed Eicher not to record the performance, his producer decided to do so anyway, just in case, and this was very much an 'in case' moment. The 'Köln Concert' became the best-selling piano solo jazz album of all time.

This idea of letting go also extends to forgetting about mistakes. Jazz great Thelonious Monk declared, 'There are no wrong notes.'[4] This advice is just as true for the veteran musician as it is for the novice. When jazz pianist Herbie Hancock played for the first time with legend Miles Davis, he almost immediately played what sounded to him like 'the wrong notes'. Mortified, and thinking that his first opportunity to play with Davis would be his last, Hancock was shocked when Davis looked at him and played those 'wrong' notes back and weaved them into his melody. It was a powerful lesson in letting go of the idea of perfection and building on any idea you're given. Even Miles Davis himself once said, 'It's not the note you play that's the wrong note. It's the note you play afterwards that makes it right or wrong.'[5]

One of the most famous examples of letting go of expertise comes from jazz saxophonist Sonny Rollins, who was already famous when he took a sabbatical at age 29 after hearing his own musical limitations and repetitions in his albums. He took three years off and played, often 15–16 hours a day, on the pedestrian walkway of the Williamsburg Bridge in Manhattan next to the subway tracks so that he wouldn't disturb a pregnant neighbour in his apartment building. When he returned to 'the real world', he released his next album, *The Bridge*, a critical and commercial hit. Listeners remarked that they didn't recognize Rollins' sound as he had so completely reinvented himself.

To illustrate and practise the beginner's mind, Steele runs an exercise in his corporate workshops where he asks someone who has no musical experience to come on stage and play with him on the keyboard, while the band will follow and perform a brand new piece. Steele suggests that there are no such things as wrong notes and that the musicians in the band can work with anything that arises, even from a beginner with no expertise whatsoever. This exercise also offers a brave volunteer the experience of feeling like a beginner again.

On one occasion, Steele recalls a woman in the audience who challenged him because she thought that such an idea was impossible and that this concept of 'beginner's mind' wouldn't and couldn't work in practice. Steele invited *her* to be the performer and, encouraged by the applause of her colleagues, the woman eventually agreed. They performed a beautiful piece and the audience gave a raucous standing ovation when they finished. When Steele asked the woman how the experience felt, she burst into tears. When she regained her composure, she reflected that she hadn't anticipated how much the band supported and built on her contributions, even though she had no idea what she was adding to the piece. She felt for the first time in a long time the freedom of expression. As Steele defined it, 'Jazz reminds people what it is to be human, reveals our inner voice and how we treat ourselves and others.'

Giving your people the opportunity to dive into the beginner's mind, no matter the medium you use, can be a powerful way to break down the mental barriers that prevent us from considering the possible. If the team works with 'what they have', with whatever stimulation their colleagues contribute, the group organically explores new directions with no expectation. One other medium that accomplishes this goal, and a near neighbour to jazz, is improvisational comedy.

Improvisation

Neil Mullarkey[6] focused on science in school, but he didn't want to wear a lab coat when he got to university so he studied Social and Political Science at the University of Cambridge. He had to take an economics class as a prerequisite. Mullarkey remembers, 'I found it interesting, but I had a frustrating experience with my supervisor. We would start our small-group discussions and he'd say, "Assume perfect competition", which economists do, and I said, "Why do you assume that? Why do you assume we're rational economic actors because I'll buy stuff from the guy I like, or the store that's near me, or I'll like the colour, or the ad will have a nice song attached or something? Nothing to do with my looking at all the prices." And he said, "No, we have to." And it was the kind of thing where all your models only work under that assumption.' Frustrated, Mullarkey became more interested in comedy and theatre outside of his studies. He joined the Cambridge Footlights sketch comedy group that has launched the careers of luminaries such as Emma Thompson, Stephen Fry, Peter Cook, Hugh Laurie, John Cleese, Sacha Baron Cohen and Olivia Colman.

After graduating from university, Mullarkey was a comedy writer and performer in London when he met an unknown Canadian comic named Mike Myers, who was in the UK for a spell to try to break into a gig at the Edinburgh Fringe Festival. Remembering the energy and spontaneous creativity of their earlier improvisation (or just 'improv') experience – Mullarkey at Cambridge Footlights and Myers at Second City in Toronto – the two founded the Comedy Store Players with Paul Merton, among others, and improv became a highlight attraction in London's Soho neighbour-hood. The troupe soon grew to include Josie Lawrence. If all those names sound familiar, it's because these were some of the first performers on British television's long-running improv series *Whose Line Is It Anyway?*. Improv is of course performing scenes with no script and no rehearsal. The actors simply start after receiving a prompt or suggestion from the audience. Listening to your partner on stage is absolutely essential.

After a decade of acting, professional comedy and improv, Mullarkey got to a point in his life where he'd be on a movie set and think, 'Who are the people who are really working and being creative here? Not that the actors weren't, but there were long periods of sitting in a Winnebago and in my case just eating cake all the time because it was free and constantly available. I looked at the director and thought, "I want to have his or her job."' So Mullarkey took a few directing courses and then looked at the producers: '*They're* busy all the time! Maybe I should do that. I took a producing course. I learned about how you finance a project, debt versus equity finance. I thought, "That's interesting. Do you borrow money? Do you get investors, but then don't you have to give them a share of the pie?" I was reading the business pages of the paper more than the arts pages and I suddenly got to the point where I had to ask, "Is that really what I want to do?" I started looking at doing an MBA. Wouldn't it be fun not to have to do any kind of show business work for a year and just read books and talk to clever people? Then my fiancée, now my wife, said, "Why would you take a year out of something you love?" And I thought, "I don't love all of it. I love the Comedy Store Players. I love doing improv. I don't love going to an audition, where the script is so often not something I want to do, or it's a commercial and they look at you straightaway and think, he's wrong, too tall, too fat, too thin."'

As a result of these reflections, Mullarkey's journey took him along a different path over the following years as he quickly identified the application of improv and intense listening to help business leaders and teams with their dynamics. Many of us have been in workshops with our teams receiving skills training from actors who have little experience of the challenges and environments of traditional industries, and those sessions are sometimes less useful than they could be since something is lost in translation. Mullarkey, however, was always fascinated with the business world and sought to bring improv as a leadership tool to a corporate environment.

At that time, Mullarkey was asked to do an improv workshop for a drama group in Bury St Edmunds, a beautiful town in Suffolk in the east of England. He found about 20 drama students there but also people doing drama as a hobby: lawyers, farmers, etc. It was just joyous for Mullarkey to see non-actors welcoming and delving into the world of improv. Mullarkey had just discovered the work of Frank Farrelly, author of a book titled *Provocative Therapy*[7] about using humour in psychological and mental health interventions. Thinking of his own upbringing, Mullarkey recalled that his father, a marketing director in the oil and gas industry, wouldn't take his job too seriously and used humour in his management style. He was always teasing that world and the pomposity of it, and Mullarkey could see that his father's colleagues loved him. He went to see Farrelly speak in the Netherlands, and many people he met there said that they were 'coaches'. Mullarkey didn't know what that meant because they weren't sports coaches but *executive* coaches. He thought, 'That's interesting. Coaching for business managers is a *thing*. I'm sure if people were coached to listen better and use humour more, they'd be both better leaders and better followers.' Mullarkey's curiosity drove him further to listen and write to other people who were delivering relevant work, and they too suggested that tools like improv had something to offer business. All these seedlings in Mullarkey's mind – what business is, what leadership is, what he and improv could bring to this world – were germinating.

Mullarkey's next step was to run a half-day improv session on a Leading Strategy and Change course at Ashridge. On day three, they simply said to the participants, 'You do it now. You organize today.' It was *that* left field! Staff at Ashridge thought improv would fit into some of what they were doing. They concluded that leadership and organizations themselves must be improvisational. No organization exists other than in the conversations of those who are in it and communicating with it dynamically. There may be a building, but it's really just a bunch of conversations, thoughts and cultures inside, like a complex improv story. In improv, though, there's an ending, usually when someone shouts, 'And – curtain!' But organizations don't have that curtain. They evolve, change and develop, and they often realize at some point that they were too late to change. Mullarkey read similar ideas from Ronald Heifetz and his theory of adaptive leadership,[8] and Ralph Stacey's theories about complexity and emergence in leadership,[9] and this is exactly what occurs in an improv scene – some things happen and then you gradually begin to realize what the scene is about. You can start with an idea and the idea may lead you to the next step, but at some point you let go.

Mullarkey was beginning to realize he had a great deal to offer, standing on the shoulders of the giants of improv combined with the philosophy and practice of psychology, and he rather liked being in a room full of accomplished business folk teaching them improv: 'We had fun, we had laughs, and they learned through laughing, and I could learn from them. They taught me how improv has so much to offer the world of business, as much as I think I taught them. I delivered workshops for Judge Business School at the University of Cambridge and for communications agency Saatchi & Saatchi. It was just this evolving thing whereby I could offer more than I realized. The peripheral elements of improv like storytelling and presentation began to loom large because the organization is a story and the leader has to be a good storyteller. When people go to presentation training, it's often more than "slow down, stand up straight, rehearse". It's "Who am I? What is my leadership role? What is my purpose?" So I would deliver a workshop for 20 people or a keynote for 400 and afterwards some people would come up and say, "Can I have a bit of one on one?"'

Now with certainty that he was onto a proposition that the world wanted and needed, Mullarkey researched a coaching course for organizational consultants at Ashridge in 2012 that looked at all different types of coaching. They introduced methods that included gestalt, psychoanalysis, cognitive behavioural therapy, but emphasized that it was all about the relationship between the coach and the client, not about sticking to one style. It's again like an improv session: 'What is this moment? How is this client? What are they telling me? What is this situation telling me?' Improv asks, 'What is the offer in the scene? What's my partner giving me and how can I build on that?' This inner dialogue is very much aligned with coaching, and Mullarkey was convinced by this time that improv and theatre had much to offer business. He was particularly excited when he read Francesca Gino's book *Rebel Talent*[10] in which she entreats the reader to 'learn everything, then forget everything'. She also introduced the concept of 'serendipity' because in nearly every art form, we welcome serendipity, found objects and mistakes.

Being open to the possible, discovering through exploration rather than planning, and letting go of control are usually not qualities that corporations either foster or encourage. Yet we know from earlier in this book that adaptability and innovation are key characteristics that CEOs claim their organizations require today more than ever. Theatre has embedded these qualities for centuries. When rehearsing Shakespeare, we put a scene on its feet because we don't quite know what Shakespeare meant in each moment, so we discover it by trying it out and then it becomes clear. Mullarkey reflects, 'From doing the scene, I discover that if I turn around just there, for example, the words make more sense. So the mistakes, the happenstance, the non-linear nature of creativity are welcomed. I come from a comedy-writing background where the sketch first seems funny, then it seems terrible, then you rewrite it and it seems ok, and you perform it and the scene is still just ok, and then you rewrite it again and it may become brilliant. It's not linear, it's kind of up and down, and it's to do with yourself too and how close you are to the piece. I've been working with improv in business for 20 years now and I observe some people are scared of improv. They think it has nothing to do with business, but it's interesting that so many of the deficits we find in many leaders can be helped through improv: collaboration, creativity and innovation, forming teams, adaptability, all of which are Improv Central. Improvisational performers like Eddie Izzard seem to have these qualities in abundance.'

If we turn to Izzard's autobiography to learn about her process, we learn that none of her stand-up material has ever been written down beforehand. It *all* started as improvisation! Izzard describes her development process in a way that I have never heard from any other comedian: 'The method I use to develop new material is what I call "verbal sculpting". I develop the shows on stage in front of a live audience. A lot of people write their stuff down and then perform it, but I still have great difficulty writing stand-up. So I don't write it down. It's the oral tradition of storytelling. Human beings have been doing it for thousands of years. Instead, I develop pieces of material and then, between those pieces, I can break off and go in a different direction. It's a bit like a jazz musician saying, "I'm going to go off on a solo here." But I haven't got a band, it's just me. All my material was improv at one point, which is why it feels like I'm making it all up. I'm not, but it is conversational. My material is loose so I can improvise on a tangent or add in a new piece whenever I want to. Even though I have a very bad processing speed (because of my dyslexia), I apparently have a large mental map.'[11]

In a similar way that Izzard identified and applied principles of improv to refine her stand-up, Neil Mullarkey uses eight principles of good improv in his leadership coaching. Though Mullarkey and I only met in the last couple of years, I found that I have used these same principles as well in my corporate work, whether explicitly named or not, drawing on my own experience of directing and performing in improv groups for a decade. They are:

1 *Yes, and…*: Explore ideas presented rather than immediately knock them down, even if that's your instinct.

2 *The offer*: Make your partner look good.

3 *Create context*: Place opportunities and challenges in the bigger picture: What are we trying to do? With whom? Where? Why? Clarity enhances enjoyment in and ability to accomplish the task.

4 *Build in structure*: As with context, creativity doesn't mean disorganized.

5 *Enhance serendipity*: Build in opportunities for people who wouldn't otherwise see one another to interact so your conversations are richer and more diverse.

6 *Storytelling*: An incredibly useful competence for leaders! This is not about innate ability but applying a framework skilfully.

7 *Practise*: All of these habits don't turn out perfectly the first time you try them. Keep practising and be comfortable with imperfection. Trust that you will refine your effectiveness as you learn and refine the habits described here.

8 *Be comfortable with not knowing*: Intolerance of failing, either personally or in one's team, is a quick road to mediocre inventiveness.

Let's explore these principles in turn:

1. Yes, and...

If my consulting and executive education experience is anything to go by, the following just may be the most valuable piece of advice in this book.

We've all been there. In the shower that morning, you have a brilliant insight and you rock up to work buzzing with anticipation to tell your boss about your genius idea. After sharing it, the boss looks thoughtful for a moment and remarks, 'Yes, but...' and your world shatters into a thousand shards of disappointment. It doesn't even matter what the boss says next. We all know that 'Yes, but...' means 'No' or even 'That's the worst idea I've ever heard, and I've heard a few'. A dreaded variation of 'Yes, but...' occurs with the preface 'With respect...', which of course means your idea is about to be thoroughly *dis*respected, and of course the prelude to the ultimate put-down is 'With the *greatest* respect...'.

As managers, we have to be wary of the insidious 'Yes, but...' which shuts down ideas before exploring them for even a moment. Over time, the surest way to shut down all creative input in a team is for the manager to act as the minister of 'Yes, but...'. Why would anyone propose a new idea if they know it's only going to be shot down immediately? The manager who is fond of 'Yes, but...' soon finds that the team will simply wait to hear their the leader's ideas and then just build on those. The creative capacity of the team has instantly shrunk from the collective brainpower of the entire team to the innovation of a single person – the leader. There's even an acronym for this dynamic: HiPPO, which stands for Highest Paid Person's Opinion, or the tendency for colleagues to defer to the most senior person in the room.[12]

Luckily, there's a very simple hack to 'Yes, but...' and it's 'Yes, and...'. Changing this one word flips the whole tenor of the conversation on its head. It encourages, builds upon and validates the idea and the colleague. Try making a habit of immediately responding 'Yes, and...' to an idea. You may not even know what you're going to say next, but that preamble programs your brain to start thinking about how the concept *might* work, or how you can go even bigger or bolder.

Remember, you don't ultimately have to implement the idea, but giving it a little airtime goes a very long way in helping your team feel engaged and valued. You may also surprise yourself about the idea's merits, which you hadn't considered until you explored it a bit. Even when you fundamentally disagree with someone, dwelling in their reality or context even for a minute or two will help them get behind whatever solution you ultimately adopt because *they feel that you listened.*[13]

After Mullarkey taught the power of 'Yes, and…' to a team at the British Broadcasting Corporation (BBC), one person said, 'I've found so many of my emails were "yes, but…".' At the BBC, a lot of people were worried that they'd come up with a turkey, so their ideas resembled the good ones they had had before but just rejigged. However, the best ideas are ones like the television series *The Office*. Where did *that* come from? That concept didn't look like other British sitcoms. The Head of Comedy at the BBC almost made a big mistake when he said, 'I like this pilot, but could we have somebody else play the character of David Brent? Maybe he doesn't have to be such a loser?' It simply wouldn't have worked without Ricky Gervais in that role, playing it the way he did. Ultimately, the BBC decided to 'yes, and…' the idea and double down on the David Brent character being cluelessly incompetent, and even more humour coming from his team being so disillusioned and disaffected as a result.

Alex Steele uses this 'yes, and…' exercise to illustrate the dynamic of accepting and building on a musical idea in jazz. When he introduced the concept to the leaders of a European clearing bank, his client later reported that everything changed after that: the culture, morale, innovation. They even correlated this difference in the top team's dynamic to profit growth.

When I introduced 'Yes, and…' to the executive team of an Antipodean mining services company, their respective departments almost immediately returned to me, demanding, 'What did you *do* to them? The difference is night and day!' Of course, the difference wasn't just that they were using the magic phrase, but the phrase triggered a different behaviour. If a leadership community is committed to a different behaviour, then the organization's culture will also de facto change.

If I've convinced you to try 'Yes, and…', may I also recommend another small behavioural shift that can have an overweighted return on the simple effort of trying something new? If you are a leader, at the beginning of a brainstorming meeting tell your team that you will not say anything until you've heard from everyone else first. In a similar way to 'Yes, and…', you're communicating that you're going to consider and value other people's opinions first, that you don't want yours to be the default option. Decision science calls this dynamic that you're circumventing the 'anchor bias'. This bias tells us that everyone's thoughts unconsciously orbit around the first idea they hear. A good analogy would be the 'guess the number of jelly beans in the jar' contest at a fair. If you are standing nearby and reading the guesses that people are writing down, your estimate will be anchored around those guesses. For example, if you see someone guess '1,000 jelly beans', you will likely compose your guess starting from the question, 'Is the right number higher or lower than a thousand?' The problem is that 1,000 may be wildly incorrect, but you've already anchored yourself in the other person's orbit whereas you may need to be in a totally different galaxy! For the leader, practising silence will allow more opinions to be surfaced and more galaxies to enter your creative universe.

2. The offer: Make your partner look good

Practise what Mullarkey calls 'intentive listening': my intention is to build on and sustain your idea rather than block it. A 'block' is an improv term for a denial rather than 'yes, and…'. Mullarkey urges his executives to think of a block as perhaps an offer in disguise, i.e. reframe it to make your partner look good.

He cites a great example of this from the early days of the Comedy Store, when Mike Myers was on stage with a fellow player. The suggestion from the audience was to hold the scene in a shop. Mullarkey recalls that the beginning of their scene went something like this:

Myers mimes wiping down the counter of his corner store. His partner in the scene walks in.

Player: Hello.

Myers: Yes, can I help you?

Player: Mmm. Yes, I was wondering if… Could I maybe take a look at that?

[Note here that the Player's suggestion, while not a block, is not helpful at first to the scene because it does not advance the who, what, where of the story or what the object in question is that he wishes to buy, which would help to define the kind of shop we're in, but Myers reframes it to make his partner's contribution look brilliant.]

Myers: Hey, it's you, Mr Vague! A pleasure to see you! I never thought you'd come to *my* shop!

Player: [Recognizing the offer] Yes, I am indeed Mr Vague. I've been vague all over the world. I've been vague in some of the best shops.

They go on with the scene and the comedy comes from all the Player's comments and suggestions being as vague and nebulous as possible. Mullarkey remembers that Myers' suggestion made the scene because he's such a generous listener, not by undermining his partner but by heightening his partner's unconscious offer. Myers said that in Hollywood, they always say, 'If you can't fix it, then feature it.'

You see that same philosophy watching Eddie Izzard do her stand-up comedy. She mumbles. She goes off point. She digresses. You would think that's terrible stand-up technique, but she made that her act through years of iteration and failure. In her memoir, she explains, 'These days when I start a new show, I begin with a whole bunch of ideas that I have written down in the Notes app on my iPhone. Then I do a series of work-in-progress gigs to try out these ideas and see if I can get them into shape. I use the audience as a script editor. Their reactions to my ideas prove whether they work or not…. And it's only because I have done it before that I believe I can do it again.'[14]

Izzard took it upon herself to host a comedy night series, and she said she ran out of material after a week. So in between the other acts, she just started chatting with the audience about what was in the room and what she felt, and that became her rhythm, meter and style. That's what improv is: What have we got here? What's this object? What has the audience given us? What have you given me? Improv actually has many meta-rules, which the audience wouldn't even be aware of, like 'yes, and…', but at its heart, improv is 'How can I make the other person look good? How can I make sure they have a good time rather than undermine their offer? How can I make everything they give me a great choice and throw it back with something from which they can make another great choice?'

Requests that Mullarkey receives from business leaders tend to be around enhancing creativity or getting along better or being more collaborative. He will often start with just a simple listening exercise. Eventually, the managers begin to realize that they're not listening fully. Mullarkey plays a one-word story game where each person contributes one word to a story in turn, such as 'I... went... to... the... zoo. I... saw... an... elephant.' And, of course, one person may be thinking 'elephant' but the other person, without even thinking, has got a giraffe in their mind. They hear 'I... saw... an...' and they can't think of something beginning with a vowel so they say 'giraffe'. That's fine. 'An giraffe' becomes a thing, that becomes a running gag, and the joy in the story may come when the giraffe and the elephant ultimately get together. As Creativity consultant Paul Plsek[15] says, 'Creativity is bringing together two hitherto unconnected ideas.' So Mullarkey will say to his clients, 'It doesn't matter if your giraffe is taken backstage now because in a minute it will meet the monkey and then what happens? What's the relationship among the giraffe, the monkey and the elephant? So practise real listening or "listening with intent", which is, "I'm intending to use something you said or something that's there to build upon." I'm aware of your assumptions.'

It isn't just luck to turn an offer into a productive response. It's a heightened awareness to be able to think, 'Oh, that's a giraffe. What can I do with a giraffe?' It isn't just 'que sera sera'. It's more like, 'I'm open to things that didn't come from the normal channels. I'm exploring my own assumptions and thinking about whether those assumptions are helping me or not.' Of course, one will always have some assumptions, but it's all about challenging those. In the last 20 years, how many assumptions have been challenged even in venerable industries? Look at Airbnb, for example – the biggest hotel company in the world, but it doesn't own any hotels. Mullarkey always tries to say to clients when they're talking about creative ideas, 'Who's eating your lunch now?' And it's not always the other hotel chain or the other carmaker.

This was brilliantly expressed when Mullarkey was consulting to a language school and asked, 'Who are the other language schools?' And they said, 'We don't care about them. We care about Airbnb because Airbnb is actually taking students away. The language school is as much an accommodation and travel enabler as it is a language enabler, and Airbnb is enabling travel and accommodation.' Airbnb is even thinking about having meetups among all its guests in San Francisco, where people can practise their English. The company is creating the same sort of social network that a language school would create.

Look at text messages on phones. Text was a kind of funny add-on that consumers realized was useful. It became so central to mobile phones for a certain generation but originally was almost an afterthought. Post-it Notes were also an afterthought, a mistake, by their clever inventor, Arthur Fry of 3M, who started using them during choir practice to keep notes without defacing the choir books. Eventually others realized the Post-it's commercial potential.

The very idea of improv revolves around taking an offer and making it look great. Mullarkey uses the example of when your partner in an improv scene might say, 'Good morning, Doctor', you're a doctor, it's the morning, and that's now the reality of the scene. Don't say, 'I'm not a doctor.' On the other hand, a great improviser might respond to that block with, 'Oh, you're *not* the doctor? Well, I'm not a patient either. Let's have fun messing around in the hospital', and they'll have a whole scene where what seemed like a block becomes entertaining to see how they cope with and build on it. A left-field offer can be joyous, unlike unfortunately in business sometimes where the grumpy guy in the corner might try to ignore the person offering different thinking: 'Oh, he's never going to play correctly. Let's just cut him out.'

Mullarkey learned at Ashridge to bring in the person who's blocking or 'yes, butting' and see that person as a left-field offer rather than as a block because, of course, if you bring them in, the change or transformation will be all the more robust if the apparent naysayer is now on board. Not only does that send a message to the others but you also might start to get the blocker to contribute their creativity too, which can be so powerful. In the business world, the offer could be what's happening in the market, consumer behaviour, technology, whatever. You can't change it, so how do you use it going forward?

3. Create context

When I studied improv at the Groundlings School of improv and sketch comedy in Los Angeles, the first commandment was 'who, what, where'. In other words, before you do anything in an improvised scene, you have to establish the architecture around which the scene is going to play out.

- *Who*: Who are you? Who is the other person? What is your relationship?

- *What*: What do you want in this scene? What will you do to get it? What are you doing in this scene?
- *Where*: Where are you? Why?

Groundlings trainers were fierce in drilling into the students that your 'who, what, where' should be set up at the very beginning of the scene, before you say or do anything else, and ideally within the first 15 seconds. In fact, we would do an exercise where that was all we would do – we would get a suggestion to begin the scene from colleagues (a location, an object, anything) and two students would set up their 'who, what where' within 15 seconds and the trainer would then stop the scene. All we were working on was scene hygiene – setting it up for success. When 'who, what, where' is executed seamlessly and quickly, both performer and audience may relax into the scene because they know the conceit, the architecture, within which the story will be told. There's little that's more annoying than watching improv when you see the performers just trying to be clever and you have no idea what the scene is about – it's just a nebulous conversation between characters whose only apparent raison d'être is to be witty.

Without knowing the 'who, what, where', an improv scene turns rancid in its ambiguity very quickly:

- *A*: Hello. Who are you?
- *B*: I'm somebody.
- *A*: Oh, look at that thing there.
- *B*: Yeah, I know.

You don't have a story! As the great novelist and screenwriter William Goldman said, 'Always start the scene as late as possible.'[16] In other words, just set it up for success first before you start exploring and playing within the groundwork that you've set. To show that contrast, a bad scene might begin:

- *A*: Oh, come in.
- *B*: Yes. Hello.
- *A*: Would you like a cup of tea?
- *B*: Yes.
- *A*: Please have a seat. Everything ok?
- *B*: Yeah.

Whereas a great scene starter is:

- *A*: I want a divorce.

Mullarkey recognizes that this is how great film editors work: 'We call that endowing somebody else with a backstory. The bizarre thing about improv is that it's spontaneous and possibly messy, but it's spontaneously trying to create structure. That's where the emergent strategy of academics like Henry Mintzberg[17] and Ralph Stacey lies. In hindsight, you could say, "Well, that was the only place we could end up", but at any point there were multiple choices. At some point, you realize the beginning rubric may not have been great but you had to go through it. So with who, what and where, you're trying to anchor.'

In the same way, creating some context before a creative brainstorming conversation at work can be incredibly helpful. I use 'who, what, where' in a very similar manner. If, for example, I'm leading a meeting where we're going to brainstorm new product ideas, I don't want to begin by just declaring, 'Ok. New product ideas – shout them out – go!' And I *have* been in such soul-destroying meetings. Instead, I need to offer a little clarity first:

- *Who*: Who are the customers we're trying to reach? Describe them. Do we currently serve them or not? What's their relationship to us or our brand?

- *What*: What type of product or service would meet an unserved or underserved need or desire?

- *Where*: Where would the customer go to find this product or service, or to find us? In a shop? What kind of shop? Or if online, what search terms or what e-commerce platforms would they use?

4. Build in structure

We should acknowledge that there is indeed structure in creativity and innovation. Mullarkey tells people, 'Improv has its own structure. I would say improv has a left-brained structure to enable right-brained creativity. So "yes, and…" is a little structure. A macro-structure is the story: you want the princess and the prince to be together; you want the dragon to be defeated; you want the treasure to be found. When we do a show, we start at the same time every Sunday, we know which games we're going to play, we have a cast, the Comedy Store takes care of insurance, lights and sound, so there is a structure within which to improvise.' In their book *Humour, Seriously*,[18] authors Jennifer Aaker and Naomi Bagdonas encourage us to create some sort of structure for levity: rituals when a project finishes, owning up to failures and making it funny, using humour as a tool for resilience, rapport and creativity. But how do we manage structure in business innovation? We usually send people away to be creative, we send them on brainstorms, we have a 'creative unit', we make them build rafts out of something, rather than ask, 'How do we make creativity part of the everyday?'

Mike Myers always drew on his Second City lessons when teaching for Comedy Store Players that a scene had to quickly have a structure. Myers would say, 'Specific, specific, specific!' Neil Mullarkey might include questions to provide structure, such as: Why have the gods of improv asked us to play this scene today? Why this hospital? Why these two people? Why this moment? Why in the morning and not the afternoon? You can never be too specific. An improv audience doesn't typically realize that the scenes they're watching are constantly trying to create structure. They're not embracing anarchy but navigating structure. Mullarkey concludes, 'Improv certainly starts with spontaneity and chaos but is always trying to bend towards structure.'

Mullarkey's point reminds me about the year I was directing my college improv group, the Yale Exit Players. I was close to a lot of improvisers in another campus troupe. Their director asked me to have lunch with him so we could compare notes about directing improv. He was a bit down about a show they had performed a few nights earlier, which I had happened to attend. He asked me what I thought about it. I told him that his players were extremely bright, funny and open actors. The issue was simply that they didn't have sufficient structure, so a scene would just explore a joke and would feel like people desperately trying to be randomly funny. The audience didn't have a story, didn't know the who, what and where: who the characters were, what they were doing, where they were, why they were together, etc.

In short, they just needed a little more discipline and, counterintuitively, the scene would feel more spontaneous, entertaining and clever.

One of the most everyday occurrences in a company is the meeting, which often doesn't create much value, but some structures in meetings can yield results whose impacts far outweigh the time invested in introducing those structures. Mullarkey often consults with businesses to make their meetings more productive: 'There are ways of creating moments where, shall we say, improv or comedy writing could work, but I also give a workshop where I just look at the mechanics: take the topic, write a hundred words to do with the topic, forget them, then list what makes me angry, what makes me happy, what's happening right now, and then gradually, gradually begin to focus on an emerging theme.'

There are other techniques that could unearth previously hidden ideas and energize the conversation:

- *Exaggerate*: Overblow the significance of what you're saying just to see if there's excitement in elements of the idea that wouldn't have been observed before.

- *Truth*: State the elephant in the room or say the idea that you would ordinarily edit or delete.

- *Distortion*: Take ideas in wholly new directions that you didn't intend in order to explore other facets or angles. You can always then pull it back. The distortion is intended to change your perception of the topic, not to converge on the practical.

- *Take something too far*: This technique is sometimes called 'nuclear escalation' in improv. Project how the smallest stimulation in a discussion can be extrapolated to its most extreme consequence, either positive or negative.

- *Notice something and express it in a way that nobody else expresses it*: Intentionally provide the perspective that no one else offers.

There are always these smaller techniques or structures that leaders can use, and there are many other macro-structures that can help put order and flow around a message. Improvisation guru and author Keith Johnstone created one such structure, which is adding 'the tilt' to a scene. In this case, the scene's going well, you've established the who, what and where, and at some point there needs to be a revelation, a switch or a pivot, which is otherwise known as the tilt. You don't want the tilt straightaway, you only want it after you've established the norm. This is classic storytelling structure. Writer, director, improviser and teacher Kenn Adams described this as 'the story spine',[19] which Pixar and Disney Animation use frequently and is similar to the Writer's Journey,[20] which in turn borrows from Joseph Campbell's Hero's Journey,[21] a classic story structure in many novels and films that identifies timeless and archetypal characters and narratives across all cultures and histories (as explained in the table).

The story spine	Structure	Function
Once upon a time... Every day...	Beginning	The world of the story is introduced and the main character's routine is established.
But one day...	The event	The main character breaks the routine.

The story spine	Structure	Function
Because of that... Because of that... Because of that...	Middle	There are dire consequences for having broken the routine. It is unclear if the main character will come out all right in the end.
Until finally...	The climax	The main character embarks upon success or failure.
And ever since then...	End	The main character succeeds or fails and a new routine is established.

Kenn Adams illustrates the story spine using the Pixar film *The Incredibles*:

Once upon a time, there was a superhero named Mr Incredible who was forced to live as an ordinary man in a society where superheroes were outlawed.

Every day, he grew more and more frustrated with his stifling, boring life.

But one day, he accepted a secret superhero job from a mysterious stranger.

Because of that, he fell into the diabolical trap of this mysterious stranger who turned out to be Syndrome, a supervillain with a long-time grudge against Mr Incredible.

Because of that, Syndrome was able to capture and imprison Mr Incredible.

Because of that, Syndrome could now put his master plan in motion by setting a giant, killer robot loose on civilization.

Until finally, Mr Incredible escaped from his prison and foiled the villain by destroying the giant, killer robot.

And ever since then, he was loved by all and able to be a superhero again.[22]

Mullarkey continues, 'Returning to the tilt, you instinctively know through rehearsal, much practice and ten thousand hours that an improv scene which is going too well has sown the seeds of its own destruction. There's a three-act structure to a good improv scene:

- *Platform*: establish the norms, the relationships.
- *Tilt*: uh oh!
- *Resolution*.

You can't just have Platform then Resolution. You can't just have Tilt then Resolution. You need Platform, Tilt, Resolution. That's a useful, simple structure to use in improv. And of course, an improviser always knows too late if they haven't done the Tilt at the right time. You only know in hindsight. That's the living, dynamic nature of improv.'

5. Enhance serendipity

Many organizations are starting to make their physical spaces more open to creativity. That could mean naming a room something fun, or it could just mean the way they lay out their offices. Pixar and DreamWorks famously have no corridors. Colleagues eat lunch together – artists with producers, software designers with custodians – not just at desks with similar people. You have to leave your dedicated space.

When Pixar Animation Studios was building its campus in Emeryville, California, Steve Jobs, who was their chairman at the time, made just one request – that the bathrooms be located only in the front lobby. In that manner, everyone, no matter their function, level or project, had to bump into each other randomly travelling to and from the bathrooms. If you think about the daily routine of a digital animator, it can be very lonely, sitting at one's desk alone all day, every day. Jobs was trying to create conversations up, down and across Pixar, in this case via the bathrooms(!), so that colleagues were having unexpected discussions all the time – some of which might influence and inspire their work in a manner that could not otherwise be carefully constructed. This was about leveraging the building's layout to engineer serendipitous opportunities.

Pixar actually went further than that, having just one central cafeteria and one small area to get breakfast cereal in the morning, all designed to enhance the same effect of serendipitous encounters. An interesting sidebar here: when summer interns were asked what they valued most about their experience at Pixar, the most popular response was 'the free cereal bar'! We should acknowledge this fact that cross-pollination, the impromptu conversation, will often lead to creativity, which formalized meetings don't always do.

The late sociologist, urbanist and journalist Jane Jacobs identified how cities are serendipity engines for humankind. Both the concentration of diverse people in a large city and the frequent opportunities for bumping into (figuratively, hopefully not literally) disparate people help engineer an environment that fosters hotbeds of innovation. She asked, 'Does anyone suppose that, in real life, answers to any of the great questions that worry us today are going to come out of homogenous settlements?'[23] There are a number of factors that Jacobs listed for enhancing serendipitous encounters, including keeping the lengths of blocks short so pedestrians will turn down more avenues rather than stick to strict routines, and ensuring clusters of buildings for different uses and economic rents so that artists, executives, students and public employees are interacting frequently and easily.[24] We see this philosophy of encouraging serendipity in how Pixar has laid out its offices.

6. Storytelling

Storytelling is an incredibly useful competence for leaders! This is not about innate ability but about applying a framework skilfully.

Mullarkey calls one of his corporate workshops 'Enrich Your Pitch', which is how to tell better stories, because he realized that improv at its heart is storytelling. It's not building gags. It's funny along the way, but ultimately you want stories. Mullarkey was invited by Unilever, the global household consumer goods company, to deliver a pilot for a week-long team workshop that was supposed to be about 'How to sell something in a short space of time'. This workshop was a moment for Mullarkey when he had to admit to himself, 'I don't know how to sell things.'

Then a friend said to him, 'Always think about your improv techniques and instead of telling them how to sell, teach them how *not* to sell.' So Mullarkey set it up as 'How not to sell badly'. He set up an improv scene, which is about doing bad selling and specifically challenging one's buyers too much. For example, 'Look here, you idiot, why aren't you selling more of my products?' By comparison, what they were being asked to do in real life would feel fairly small or achievable. The exercise is akin to an athlete harnessing weights to their body while training so that in the real race they feel light and easy. Mullarkey's friend helped him by encouraging, 'Push it too far, which helps them know how to come back.' After that, Mullarkey thought, 'I can teach anybody anything if I make it into an improv exercise!'

Mullarkey utilized many other improv techniques for the workshop, but that first time he was still a little nervous telling people how to sell. When he arrived at the venue, he sat over breakfast with his client and all the participants and they listened to a really boring PowerPoint speech. Mullarkey thought, 'Oh no, I've got to warm them up after this!' So he said to everyone, 'Ok, let's go into a different room. Everyone stand up now.' When they went to the other space, he improvised and said, 'Everyone just move about, point at stuff and say things,' which is actually an improv exercise. You point at things and call them what they are: table, chair, etc. Then you have to point at something and call it the previous thing to which you pointed. So you'd point at a table, then a chair and say 'table' when pointing at the chair. It's harder than it sounds! Next, he asked them to point at things and call them anything except what they really are: 'flower, chicken, giraffe...' The participants realized that they immediately started using patterns or genres for everything they said. For example, they latched onto calling everything a fruit: 'apple, pear, banana....' They were trying to create structure amidst spontaneity.

After the first exercise, Mullarkey said, 'Let's do stories. Tell me stories about your lives.' He used a great exercise from improv author Keith Johnstone in which I tell you a story and you tell it back to me as if it happened to you. It's a great game because no one worries if it's a bad story, and actually there are no bad stories. If I'm telling the story as if it happened to me, I'm kind of relieved of any fear that I would have with a normal presentation where I'm the director, the actor, the writer. But if I'm telling a story that belongs to somebody else, I want to make it good for them. I've imbibed it. I've put it in my own words. One Unilever colleague told his story brilliantly and the group was very moved by it. Mullarkey had to remind the audience, 'This isn't *his* story. He's borrowed it from somebody else.'

Then he said to this sales manager, 'Ok, tell me about a product you're working on,' and he was dull as dishwater! Mullarkey challenged, 'Why can't you bring the power of that semi-improvised story you got from your friend to your work? Just think about that product you're working on and now cut it down. I'm only going to give you 90 seconds. You want to give me 90 slides but give me 90 seconds.' This guy thought about it for quite a while and then he spoke. 'Every year, 2 million children under the age of five will die because they don't wash their hands. They'll die of diarrhoea. What do children want? They want something fun and something quick. They want to wash their hands quickly and go away, but they want something fun. So, perhaps if they can wash their hands in 20 seconds, the soap will change colour to tell them they've spent enough time scrubbing. They won't die of diarrhoea and they can go play. And that is why we've invented Lifebuoy,[25] which is soap for life.' This was a product that Unilever debuted in 2013 in India and it was a huge success.

The audience all felt a tingle as he told that story. Mullarkey pointed out to them that it was a fairly short story. It wasn't short of hard data: 2 million children, under the age of five, 20 seconds. But he told a specific story and the power of that story helped Mullarkey to conclude, 'I can in fact teach pitching skills.' That moment stayed with him, and particularly that the story was successful because the sales-person boiled it down to the essentials. He didn't talk about the chemistry of the soap; he didn't talk about the fragrance; he didn't talk about the packaging; he didn't talk about the consumer research. He talked about issues of which we are aware and feel we can do something about them. He got to the big 'why' rather than listing product features. Mullarkey's job was to help him get to that destination. That Unilever pilot became a series of workshops across four continents, and in every place, story was the international language. The workshops revealed that salespeople are inclined incorrectly to talk about the features rather than the benefits, which Mullarkey has since discovered is a key sales maxim: 'Don't tell me what's in it. Tell me what's in it for me.' That was a powerful moment when he learned that improv, and specifically storytelling, can indeed be a key competence for managers.

7. Practise

All of these habits don't turn out perfectly the first time you try them. Keep practising, and be comfortable with imperfection.

Mullarkey's daughter was learning to play the piano. The teacher once called him in after a lesson and said, 'Your daughter's getting all the notes right, but she hasn't got the crazy.' And this was Mozart she was playing! The teacher meant that she hadn't internalized the piece to make it 'hers' or found the thing that lifted it. Mullarkey learned some-thing new about classical music in that moment. He had pre-viously assumed, 'It's the same every time, isn't it?' And then he realized that there are conductors, and they're individuals, and you've got to listen to the whole, and each conductor interprets it slightly differently: 'They're not just keeping the rhythm. There's something else. That's what I find with people who very quickly want to give up because it's going badly. I'll say, "If it's going too well too early, it might end badly."'

You get better by practising improv over and over in the same way as playing a sport. Mullarkey likens it to football: 'You might conclude: "You get the ball into the net. It's the same every time, isn't it?" Well, there are a million ways of doing it, of building up to it. So you rehearse improv to get to know the rhythms, metre, relationships, status, physicality. You learn it's powerful to take pauses, to not get to the answer too quickly. But on the other hand, in creative pursuits like music or theatre, you fail and iterate, fail and iterate. The scene's not going well; you can't learn the piece? You don't give up. You know that's a necessary process.' What business calls failure and iteration, performing arts call rehearsal.

8. Be comfortable with not knowing

Management theorist Ralph Stacey posited that there is a spectrum of uncertainty.[26] He writes that at some point the leader really does know the answer. They've been there. It's an easy question. They can cope with it. And then at some point you move into a place where the leader is asking the questions and acknowledging they don't know the answers.

MIT Professor Don Sull has a book called *The Upside of Turbulence*[27] in which he compares improv, software development (now known as 'agile') and special forces in the military such as Navy SEALs and the SAS. When you're in the special forces, you may come up against a thick wall that you have to get through. The normal, conventional, corporate idea would be: 'Thick wall – have to get to the other side. Let's start digging through it. At any point we can report back to the head office that we are X per cent through the wall and made so much linear progress.' Special forces would go, 'Hang on. This wall is really thick, but somewhere there's a vulnerability.' So they look for the hole or crack. At any point, if they have to report back to their commander, they may have to say, 'Zero per cent progress on getting through the wall,' but at some point they get to the vulnerability and they're through, zero to 100 per cent immediately. The Navy SEAL approach is perhaps more dangerous because there will be times when they have to say, 'We haven't got anywhere at all. We haven't solved it.' But they're more likely to achieve sudden, exponential results.

Of course, there are many stories of ideas that didn't work. Mullarkey always tries to temper his consulting with, 'This is all very well for me. I'm an improv guy. I do comedy. I can say silly or rude things onstage. Everyone goes home. No problem. I'm not answerable to shareholders. I'm not spending a hundred million to find the product didn't work. When I say, "Encourage failure, encourage risk," I can say that because I don't have much at risk. The audience has come to see a comedy show, whereas corporate people will have to go out on a limb. I understand that. So at some point, we can say, "This isn't quite working, so we'll throw in the Tilt. We'll find a whole new way," or we'll say, "And… curtain!" That's leadership, when you have the courage to say, "I can't see this going anywhere," versus "I can see this working." It's hard to know whether that's a structural or a personal thing. When do you say that this team, this individual or this structure is right, or it's not working? So I stress that my executive groups should take on board what I'm saying but lightly, acknowledging that they're in a different world.'

There was an experiment with jazz musicians where they had an MRI scan while they were playing, and the parts of their brain that seemed to shut down when improvising were the ones responsible for thoughts such as 'I know where it came from' and 'I care what people think'.[28] So when you see a great improv show, you might see people on stage looking as if their inner monologue is, 'What?! Did I just say that? I don't know where it came from. That's kind of embarrassing. I didn't mean to say that.' Because they're in this sacred place of vulnerability in improv, where they're allowed to be fragile, mistaken and reveal themselves, the audience doesn't mind if they end up saying weird things. It's happened to Mullarkey so many times: 'Once I couldn't remember the word "stalactite", so I said something else and of course that wrong word became part of the unfolding story.' That sudden surprise becomes the spine and it has much in common with what University of Houston Professor Brené Brown[29] says about vulnerability as a source of creativity and leadership. That's not generally where Western discourse places leadership, which is typically around power and knowing. Of course, that's why we might want to embrace more warmly Francesca Gino's entreaty to 'learn everything then forget everything'.

London Business School Professors Rob Goffee and the late Gareth Jones described the power of vulnerability in authentic leadership in their book *Why Should Anyone Be*

Led By You?.[30] A sort of rude, provocative question! One of the characteristics that the authors recommend the authentic leader to practise is the revelation of weakness. The problem with leaders trying to come across as perfect is that everyone knows that they're not, so they are instantly downgraded in their followers' perception as insincere. Of course, there's an element of skill involved in selecting weaknesses that one is comfortable to communicate. Those weaknesses must be real rather than fabricated, and allowable, meaning that they can't be faults which would erode confidence in one's effectiveness. For example, it would probably be a bad idea for a chief financial officer to reveal that they can't read a balance sheet! In a similar manner, the improviser who embraces faults and missteps in a scene is in turn embraced by the audience, assuming that the performer shows they are comfortable doing so.

As soon as an audience recognizes that one is relaxed, comfortable and confident on stage, laughing off miscues and rolling with the punches, then the audience relaxes too and goes along for the ride. In contrast, if the improvisers come across as nervous and hard on themselves, the audience is on edge with and for the actors on stage, and it's much harder for the audience members to enjoy themselves. The comparative lesson for business is that the leader must not only acknowledge their own weaknesses but encourage the team to embrace faults, mistakes and weaknesses in the creative process. The pursuit of perfection is a common adage in business, and we even see variations of this idea in many companies' values and beliefs, but it's less helpful in fostering a culture of creativity.

Tesco

I know from personal experience, having performed and directed in improv groups, that there is much that business can learn from these techniques. One of my success stories is a workshop that I delivered between 2007 and 2008 for two different teams belonging to global retailer Tesco that was completely organized around improvisational exercises. We didn't even tell participants what they would be doing when they showed up at a London West End theatre, the Royal Court, in the morning.

One of the team leaders, Emily Shamma, was Tesco's Head of Local Sourcing at the time. She recalls, 'My 20-person team was composed of representatives to local food businesses, farmers and micro-enterprises, advising small suppliers to be strong enough to provide their goods to Tesco. We were the regional face of Tesco with niche jobs in this massive organization, and one of the most entrepreneurial groups. I got to handpick every member of my team, and I recruited for innovation, creativity, charm and intelligence. We were a remote team scattered around regional offices. We were virtual before virtual was a thing.'[31] Finally coming together in person in London, Shamma wanted a purely creative and fun day that allowed for a lot of bonding and would further develop those social skills and draw them out in a manner which encouraged people to be vulnerable and try things, but also to relax into the enjoyment of the day.

Only when the team was sitting in the theatre did we tell them what we were going to do for the day. I must admit some of them looked horrified. But after no more than an hour, everyone, and I do mean everyone, was relaxed,

enjoying and revelling. By the end of the day, they were buzzing with energy and excitement, open to new avenues of how
they could tackle challenges and opportunities creatively and
collaboratively. The day consisted of a number of improv
exercises on the stage, all allowing people to explore different aspects of their personalities, 'yes, and...' ideas, even
crazy ones, lots of listening and suggesting, and making their
partners look good. A great deal of the success of the day was
not down to the games themselves but to practising the art
of gradual risk-taking. In other words, we did not have them
do full scenes in front of one another until the very end of
the day. For the entire morning, everyone performed the
exercises in pairs and trios all at once. There was no audience
to impress, only skills and stories to practise and explore.
Each successive game was just a little more difficult than the
previous one. So before they knew it, the team was doing full
games you'd see from a professional troupe, though no one
at the beginning of the day would have thought that outcome possible.

Acting out of character gives licence to be silly. Shy members of the team came out. Being at the Royal Court Theatre
forced everyone to project – yes, as performers, but also to
heighten their personalities as human beings. A big element
that made the day successful was having the workshop occur
on the stage itself. It was so important to get out of the corporate space. Shamma explains, 'In the past when we were
able to assemble the team, I always thought carefully about
the location and matching that to the theme or discussion I
wanted to have. For example, we'd meet at a supplier's farm,
maybe even in a field, or in one of our stores where we'd
walk around and say what we observed and suggest improvements, or we'd sit on the floor and draw our ideas as a big

collage. I'd do anything to get the team's mind out of "business as usual" by selecting the space because I've found that creative meetings in a board room around a whiteboard rarely work well.'

When the day with Shamma's team finished, they all had dinner together that night and everyone was relaxed, happy and proud of what they had done and the risks they had taken. Shamma knew it had been a successful investment of time: 'The day brought us closer together as a team because we were vulnerable and brave. That alone made it worthwhile. Personally, I got to know them better and they got to know me more. Even though we were acting on stage, we had to be more authentic at the same time. That's one of the most interesting creative juxtapositions. Over the following days, I observed a number of behaviours that told me the day was a success. People were more open to revealing different aspects of their personalities. They appeared more confident and had more presence. They were less afraid to speak up, speak truth to power, including to more senior colleagues and in management and board meetings.'

Improvisation is an oft-overlooked skill which even a company as traditional as a grocer could find not only useful but invaluable in the dramatic shifts in its people's capabilities. Corporations are fond of touting their adaptability skills, but when we dig down, we usually find these same companies' leaders have massive blocks when it comes to their own agility. And it makes sense. We've been conditioned to value experience, precedent and wisdom in our leaders. Of course, those are wonderful attributes to possess, but they can become weaknesses when those same leaders are confronted with challenges and dynamics, be they internal or external, that they have never encountered before. In which case, we ought to seek competencies such as comfort with ambiguity, the ability to embrace not knowing, listening, responding to one's environment, and more than a little 'yes, and…' from our leaders today. Jazz and improvisation both welcome and develop these translatable abilities for us, no matter our industry or function.

One thing you can do on Monday morning

This section is more than 'one thing' but a number of exercises, a playbook if you will, that you can run with your teams to challenge, adjust and improve team creativity, comfort with change and explore when we don't have *the* answer. We used many of these games with the Tesco teams described earlier.

What's in the box?

This is a brainstorming technique that rewards volume over quality or judgement. Explain to the team that we're going to identify as many solutions to a problem or opportunity as possible. Put the team in pairs. The pair should be standing up. You propose the question for the team to work on, such as:

- How might we attract more customers to our store?
- How do we reduce our energy costs?
- What other flavours of doughnut should we make?

In each pair, the first person's job is to invent as many solutions to the question as possible. With each answer, they reach down into an invisible box and pull out the solution. Physically reaching for the answer helps the brain to come up with the next answer on cue and reduces the instinct to pause and think, repressing the creative flow.

The second person's job is to write down what the other person says and encourage them, *always* encourage them: 'Amazing idea! What else do you have? Oh, brilliant! Can we think of more?' This is actually a tough job too because this colleague has to write down what they're hearing and respond with encouragement at the same time.

The facilitator should set and announce a time limit, such as two to three minutes, then ask the pairs to switch roles and repeat the exercise. Collect everyone's lists, and you will be amazed how many ideas you will have to explore in more detail.

One-word story

This game explores possible futures or scenarios but prevents any single person in the team from forcing a focus or direction. Ask three to five people in your team to sit or stand in a row. Pose a question to them, such as:

- What will our new branding be?
- What will be the next window display in the store?
- What will be our most popular product or service in five years?

Then your group answers the question but one word at a time and in order, going back to the first person after the last person in line has spoken. The group can tell their story for as long as you or they like. They may run out of steam or reach a natural ending. Since each person is contributing only one word in every three to five, the participants inevitably surprise themselves, exploring novel directions and possibilities. No one can dominate the direction in which the team members go with their story.

This is a little more advanced, so I encourage practice. Try it a few times, maybe once a week, communicating that there's no bad story and no bad answer or word. The only thing to ask is that people don't pause and think about their word. Instead, they just say the first word that pops into their head. Do this a few times and you'll witness that the stories will become more cogent and run for longer periods of time. The team will stop judging themselves and just get into the flow and have fun with exploring. Of course, this requires the leader to be uncompromisingly positive and non-judgemental.

And even better...

This is a game of escalation that is a good option if you want to brainstorm more elaborated, new solutions. It's a variation of 'yes, and…' and is usually played in groups of two to four. Questions could include topics such as:

- What would happen if we opened an office in Germany?
- What if we allowed customers to make up their own cocktail recipes at the bar?

Pose your question and the first person will start to invent a scenario. Let them speak for about 15 seconds. Then cue the second person, who needs to continue where the first person left off. They should start their explanation by saying, 'And even better…' Because of that prefacing statement, the scenario quickly escalates. Within five to eight speakers, you typically will have either achieved world peace or solved world hunger! But if you then look back to two or three statements before that conclusion, you might have uncovered some advantages or implications that you hadn't considered previously and might make the idea much more intriguing and worth exploring further.

If I were…

In this exercise, you do not explore an idea through the lens of your own organization or context but through another which you deeply admire. For example, instead of asking, 'How should we launch this soft drink brand in Amsterdam?', you might ask, 'If I were Richard Branson, how would I launch this drink brand in Amsterdam?' Now you've unlocked the restrictions the unconscious places around you. You might now brainstorm as if possessed:

- We'll create a surf machine in an Amsterdam canal and the surfers will be drinking the soda and wearing branded bathing suits!

- During a warm summer week, we'll give all the Amsterdam street musicians a bucket of our sodas on ice, which will encourage pedestrians to stop, enjoy a free drink, listen to the music and pay the performer.

- We'll give away branded beverage holders to Amsterdam bicycle owners, which is basically everyone!

Brainstorming through the perspective of another person or company frees your creativity, unburdened with your or your organization's assumptions about 'how we do things around here'. All of a sudden, you find yourself considering ideas or actions that you never would have entertained before.

Endnotes

1 Interview with Alex Steele, 10 August 2020.

2 Shunryu Suzuki, *Zen Mind, Beginner's Mind* (Boulder, CO: Shambhala Publications, Anniversary Edition, 2020).

3 Don Heckman, 'Pianist Keith Jarrett: The story of the Köln Concert', Grammys, 15 May 2017, https://www.grammy.com/grammys/news/pianist-keith-jarrett-story-k%C3%B6ln-concert (archived at https://perma.cc/VR4J-8V2X)

4 Rhona-Mae Arca, 'There's no such thing as a wrong note', Musespeak Studio blog, 18 December 2008, https://www.musespeak.com/blog/2008/12/theres-no-such-thing-as-a-wrong-note.html (archived at https://perma.cc/HWV2-JN32)

5 Ibid.

6 Interview with Neil Mullarkey, 31 July 2020.

7 Frank Farrelly, *Provocative Therapy* (Meta Publications, 1989).

8 Ronald Heifetz, Marty Linsky and Alexander Grashow, *The Practice of Adaptive Leadership* (Boston: Harvard Business Review Press, 2009).

9 Ralph Stacey, *Tools and Techniques of Leadership and Management: Meeting the Challenge of Complexity* (Abingdon: Routledge, 2012).

10 Francesca Gino, *Rebel Talent: Why It Pays to Break the Rules at Work and in Life* (New York: HarperCollins, 2018).

11 Eddie Izzard with Lauren Zigman, *Believe Me: A Memoir of Love, Death, and Jazz Chickens* (London: Penguin Random House, 2017), 294–295.

12 https://whatis.techtarget.com/definition/HiPPOs-highest-paid-persons-opinions (archived at https://perma.cc/TY93-M3NB)

13 Patrick Lencioni, *The Five Dysfunctions of a Team* (Hoboken, NJ: John Wiley & Sons, 2002).

14 Eddie Izzard with Lauren Zigman, *Believe Me: A Memoir of Love, Death, and Jazz Chickens*.

15 Paul Plsek, www.directedcreativity.com (archived at https://perma.cc/USL4-L9D8)

16 Michael Schilf, 'Scenes: Start late, get out early', thescriptlab.com (archived at https://perma.cc/TJ33-2NXV), 11 June 2010.

17 Henry Mintzberg, *The Rise and Fall of Strategic Planning* (Upper Saddle River, NJ: Prentice Hall, 2000).

18 Jennifer Aaker and Naomi Bagdonas, *Humour, Seriously* (London: Portfolio Penguin, 2020).

19 Kenn Adams, 'Back to the story spine', Aerogramme Writers' Studio, 5 June 2013, https://www.aerogrammestudio.com/2013/06/05/back-to-the-story-spine/ (archived at https://perma.cc/L69F-KTS6)

20 Christopher Vogler, *The Writer's Journey: Mythic Structure for Storytellers and Screenwriters* (London: Boxtree Ltd, 1996).

21 Joseph Campbell, *The Hero with a Thousand Faces* (Novato: New World Library, 3rd Edition, 2012).

22 Kenn Adams, 'Back to the story spine'.

23 Jake Dobkin, 'Stephen Goldsmith, editor of *What We See*', Gothamist.com, 14 May 2010, https://gothamist.com/arts-entertainment/stephen-goldsmith-editor-of-emwhat-we-seeem (archived at https://perma.cc/K9QS-4R2Z)

24 Jane Jacobs, *The Death and Life of Great American Cities* (London: Random House, 50th Edition, 2011).

25 Unilever, 'The Hulk of handwashes', Unilever.com, 3 August 2013, https://www.unilever.com/news/news-and-features/Feature-article/2013/the-hulk-of-handwashes.html# (archived at https://perma.cc/NKN8-9WTV)

26 www.gp-training.net/uncertainty-complexity-chaos-risk/complexity-stacey-matrix/ (archived at https://perma.cc/6TND-A7ZA)

27 Don Sull, *The Upside of Turbulence: Seizing Opportunity in an Uncertain World* (New York: HarperCollins, 2009).

28 Johns Hopkins Medical Institutions, 'This is your brain on jazz: Researchers use MRI to study spontaneity, creativity', *Science Daily*, 28 February 2008, https://www.sciencedaily.com/releases/2008/02/080226213431.htm (archived at https://perma.cc/X2AS-X9ZR)

29 Brené Brown, www.brenebrown.com (archived at https://perma.cc/8SH5-26QY)

30 Rob Goffee and Gareth Jones, *Why Should Anyone Be Led by You?* (Boston: Harvard Business Review Press, 2019).

31 Interview with Emily Shamma, 1 June 2022.

04
Opening the door to inspiration
The realm of writing

Most writers with whom I've spoken share that they have to generate and sort through lots of ideas first in order to land on a great one. The same is true of business: in order to discover a ground-breaking idea, you typically need first to produce a large number of suggestions. The problem is that in contemporary corporate life we have an intense phobia of failure, which means we try to produce just the one winning idea and spend a lot of time on risk analysis and execution planning for that one concept before we decide it's not a supernova idea and try to invent another one. That's not a recipe for innovative success. So let us peer into the world of writing and the humility required to encourage many ideas before landing on the right one.

We will dive into a fascinating discussion with Andrew Reich, one of the show runners (head writers) and executive producers of hit TV series *Friends*, unpicking how he led the writers' room and his own writing process in order to solicit ideas to proliferate and respond to the other writers. This approach required his writers to hold their ideas lightly, to seek rather than tolerate feedback, and to change their environment when they felt stuck.

We'll then explore another perspective on leading a writers' room, with all its parallels with leading any innovation process, from creative polymath Arvind Ethan David who is an author, escape room impresario, and Broadway, television and film producer.

Andrew Reich

Reich's professional journey started with learning improvisation in a high school drama class.[1] He recalls, 'That just lit my brain up. I loved playing those improv games and was good at them. My teacher then took my best friend and me to other schools to teach improv. He would talk about improv and then we would demonstrate it. So when I entered Yale University, I wanted to keep doing that. I auditioned and got into the university's original improv group, The Exit Players.[2] By my second semester, I was directing the troupe and continued doing so for the rest of my college career. That collaborative creativity, listening and being in the moment in a scene, turned out to be the perfect training for being a television comedy writer.' Reich had done a little bit of writing here and there in college, but it wasn't until he started writing with roommate and fellow Exit Player Ted Cohen that the collaboration really allowed them actually to finish scripts. The process was a lot like doing improv. When they'd pitch ideas, it felt like performing scenes. One would say something and the other would have the punchline. After college, the two ended up getting an agent and some writing jobs. Eventually they were hired on *Friends*, where they stayed for seven years and worked their way up to executive producers. Since *Friends*, Reich has pitched and sold many shows, got a couple more on the air and was the show runner (the chief creative voice of the series) for those.

A TV comedy writers' room can be such an incredibly collaborative experience. There are differences in the norms of how television episodes are written among different countries. In the United States, one person usually writes an initial draft script of an episode, but the beats and stories in that script are ultimately written and reworked by the room as a whole. Reich's improv background – the listening, the 'yes, and…' and all of it – was on point for succeeding in a comedy writers' room. You inhabit all of the characters at different times. You need to be able to speak in their voices as if you were in their scenes, so Reich's training prepared him for that.

Reich also found that having that dialogue with a writing partner was much more effective than sitting at a desk by himself. Motivation is built in; the partnership makes you show up every day. Just saying things out loud, throwing out ideas and receiving feedback are processes that you don't get when it's in your head. With comedy, it's nice to make the other person laugh and you often need that stimulus and immediate response. Reich recalls that a number of stories emerged from mishearing something. You mishear what someone said but that suddenly becomes an idea, so voicing a thought and reacting increases the total volume of ideas.

Reich found the best way of working with Cohen was to take long walks together, and he still finds walking to be incredibly crucial to creativity. There's all the science of left brain–right brain behind it, but for Reich and Cohen it was just the walking and not having to sit at a table staring at each other. They found the process easier, looking all around rather than just at the other person's face, and somehow there was less pressure because they were surrounded by stimuli. J J Abrams and Lawrence Kasdan did the same when writing *Star Wars: The Force Awakens*: 'Abrams and Kasdan took long walks to talk about the script and taped their conversations... What they came up with wasn't the result of locking themselves in a room with a few pads of paper and a computer, at least at first. "He kept his iPhone with the recorder on and we'd walk," remembers Kasdan. "We'd walk for miles and miles." Because of the film's pre-production, these walks took place all over the world. "It felt good to be in motion, because so much of the movie is in motion," said Abrams.'[3]

That said, there are distinct parts of the writer's job and the environment often changes depending on what stage they're in. Reich thought that the walks were most helpful when coming up with pilots (new shows) or ideas. He remembers, 'The first time we really got together to work on our very first spec script, we went to Zuma Beach and we walked for hours. By the end of that walk, we basically had the outline for what we were going to write. Those questions at the point of a show's origin are so difficult to answer. I'm working with two women on a pilot right now. We spent months and finally pitched it for the first time to a production company. In that pitch, I was thinking, "Oh God, I thought we had it, but we just don't have it!" Even with all my experience, there were still basic questions unanswered and that's partly because there are *so many* questions that you have to answer for a show. You have a lot of ideas for shows, but sometimes an idea is just a setting, a milieu. It may feel like a great idea, such as thinking of a certain work-place that's full of comic potential, but that's often not what you need. So then you come up with a character who really wants something and has a clear obstacle in the way, and *that's* what you need. And because you need many different things to make a show work, sometimes you have a couple of the elements that you're really excited about but you can't figure out why it's not coming together. It's because you have some of the necessary elements but you're missing these other ones that are much more necessary.'

Once you're working on a show that's been commis-sioned, a writers' room is its own thing and its own environ-ment. When Reich and Cohen were hired first as writers then as executive producers (or head writers) on *Friends*, Reich recalls fondly that there were endless great creative moments in that writers' room of about a dozen people because it was just a bigger version of two people bouncing ideas around. Each character has to be fleshed out and brought to life in each distinct scene, but sometimes you can lose the big-picture questions like, 'Why should I tune in next week?' Nevertheless, when you have an existing show, the charac-ters have been created and the template is there, things just get easier at that point, or as Reich clarifies, 'Not *easy*, but you already have the story engines, what makes the show tick.'

While making a strong case for having a number of brains working on a concept, Reich also suggests that there are trade-offs when the number becomes too large, and one might by necessity have to divide the team into smaller groups to finish all the tasks to deadline. The dozen writers on staff at *Friends* could be too unwieldy all collaborating in one room, so the team would usually be split into at least two or three rooms. Shrinking budgets across the industry means that having 12 writers on a sitcom staff is rare today. The nice thing about having 12 people is that you can have 3 rooms with a good minimum of 3 people in a room. In that manner, at least 3 people are off writing a draft of an episode at any given time. While one room is writing this week's show, you already have 2 teams that are working on next week's episode and the week after. You have all these scripts that are at various stages and they all need attention. If everyone is focused on just the current week, then who's working on next week? It's nice when you can have enough people to be able to split the drafts. *Friends* was a 24-episode season. These days, a season may be 6 to 10 episodes. A typical US season is becoming more like the length of a UK season, so now you may have more time in pre-production when you can get more of the episodes written before you start shooting, which is always good.

Reich recollects, 'We couldn't always divide and conquer on *Friends*. We had cases when we had a table read (a readthrough of a full episode with the cast) and the script fell apart and needed a huge rewrite. In those cases, maybe we'd say, "OK. This room's going to work on the A story and this room will work on the B story of this episode. Then we'll read through and work on them all together." In those cases, we'd have multiple rooms working on the same episode, but the rooms are working on discrete tasks. A typical sitcom will have three stories or plots running through an episode, hence "A story, B story, C story".'

In the same way in a corporate context, it can be productive to split up a team into subgroups to tackle different facets of a problem or opportunity. Just like in a large writers' room, a company leader might discover that there are just too many heads bending to the same macro-challenge. Once an overall direction is set, the problem can often be parsed into sub-questions and smaller groups tasked to answer each question. Even when a team breaks into subgroups, each of those groups still benefits if there is a nominated leader. There always has to be someone who is moderating the discussion. If the team is splitting up, there still needs to be a chain of command where someone is running each room.

There were times when *Friends* had four show runners. Two show runners might be in the same room and in that case they'd just decide who was running the room because it's good to have someone making final decisions. The team might all be pitching different funny lines and often there would be clear consensus that one line was the best one and it was not hard to agree. But sometimes a judgement call needed to be made when someone has to say, 'OK, that line's going in.' At that point, you don't want two people arguing over it. Reich has been in the position of leading a writers' room for a long time and he likens the job to being almost like a coach rather than a player. It can be a bit of both, but ultimately you're setting the tone and are responsible for the show as a whole.

Reich says, 'You may not always be the one to pitch a line or idea because you're really trying to get the best out of your people and be clear about what you're looking for. You're really trying to keep the big picture. I find myself saying things like, "That's funny, but it's not doing what we need it to do. This line needs to do three things: it needs to get this piece of exposition out, advance this story point and give the punchline in this bit of dialogue." The other people in the room may protest, "I'm just trying to say something funny!"

Everyone's ego is on the line when they're pitching a joke and they can't help that fact. As the leader, when you're calling balls and strikes, you have to do it in a way that doesn't shut someone down for the rest of the day because they feel crushed. I find it helpful both for me and for the other person to say something like, "That's not right and this is why." It might be that it's the wrong attitude for the character, or it's not hitting the story beat, or it's not communicating this important element of the character's backstory that we have to relate in this scene. I'm actually trying to refine more clearly for *everyone* what I'm looking for, and I also want to keep people in a cheery, good mood for creativity. At the same time, if I spend too much time explaining, I'm running up against the pressure cooker that we have to get to a certain place by the end of the writing session, and as the show runner I also have to be in casting, and I'm being called down to the stage to watch a rehearsal, and I have to be in the editing room, and the network's calling asking for the next outline. I'm torn in a million different directions. But when everyone in that writers' room is tense and clenched, that's when you're most likely to yank on that *one* door and keep pulling. So I have to keep this fragile dynamic functioning as best I can, keeping in mind the big picture of the show and the purpose of the scene we're discussing.'

Belbin's team role theory posits that every team should have specific roles that each team member explicitly plays and everyone knows the role that each is playing.[4] The role of show runner that Reich describes is what Belbin would call the Coordinator's job. In this role you moderate the discussion and you are responsible for the effectiveness of the team since everyone else is focused on the task. As Reich says, his role is to draw out the best in everybody and ensure that each person has a voice, while also steering which ideas to keep and develop. In a dynamic where you're trying to maximize creativity, the Coordinator's role is perhaps the most important in a team because that person is responsible for ensuring that the group's outputs exceed those that any one individual could produce on their own. The creative team's leader is not always the font of innovative ideas but must ensure that the environment and dynamic that they create are the most fertile for innovation to occur.

Getting unstuck

Reich believes that the biggest question in creativity is, 'What do you do when you're stuck?' As such, he has thought about and practised a number of techniques in leading the creative process in his writing teams that would apply to any function or industry. We'll look at each one individually, but Reich's overall toolkit to getting a team unstuck is:

1 Provide the big picture.
2 Don't keep yanking on the door if it won't open.
3 Role model vulnerability.
4 Start with the obvious.
5 Change feeling.
6 Change environment.
7 Embrace the misery.

1. Provide the big picture

The show runner, like Belbin's Coordinator, also has the job of noting when the group is stuck and changing the approach.

Reich explains how he would lead this dynamic: 'A lot of scenes are really easy to write because they've been set up correctly; the dynamics and stakes are all there. However, sometimes on *Friends* we'd have a more radical idea for a scene, but then we wouldn't want to pursue it because it would change so much of what we'd already done and that would mean so much work. My role would be to encourage the room to explore the idea that rethinks the whole scene because maybe in fact it doesn't; maybe we can salvage more than we think. Or often when a scene isn't working, I sometimes had to ask, "Is there some fundamental problem with this scene? We think we just can't come up with this line, but is there a bigger problem? Does this scene not actually serve a purpose in the script? Is it not needed? Or does no character want anything, so there are no stakes?" I started asking fundamental questions rather than getting everyone so stuck on finding the right line or using the right prop. Maybe none of these ideas feels funny not because of the specific wording of the joke but because the whole thing is wrong. It's wrong on a character level, or it's wrong on a story level.'

Reich encouraged the team in these cases to take a step back and see the forest for the trees. It's amazing how often a team just gets stuck trying to nail a specific aspect and their focus is totally off. If Reich was not doing his job of keeping a higher-level perspective, a whole group of people could spend hours without realizing that they had gone down a rabbit hole, which can happen frequently. Reich also tried to nominate others in the room who were skilled at identifying where problems might really lie and proposing solutions.

2. Don't keep yanking on the door if it won't open

Reich describes a metaphor that's often in his brain when he's in a writers' room: 'You're in a hallway full of a lot of doors. Sometimes it feels like you're pulling on this door, just trying to yank *that* door open. And someone points out, "Guys, if we just walk down the hall a little bit, there are all these other doors. We could try those." It's amazing how many times everyone gets stuck pulling on that same door. When it's happening, you're all so focused on cracking this thing. The more people you have, the more likely you'll have someone say, "OK, wait a minute. Let's find a totally different door and see if that works." Sometimes you're reluctant to do that because there's something about what you're sure is behind your door. There's something you're attached to and you don't want to let go. But a lot of times you have to let go of that because it's not getting you anywhere. Having a few more people just increases the chance that someone's going to say, "I've got it. It's just over here, guys. We're just looking in the wrong place." I still really love that collaboration and just being able to throw something out that sparks and ask, "OK, what if they don't do that but do *this* next?"'

3. Role model vulnerability

As a writer on episodic television, writer's block is a luxury that Reich cannot afford. He says, 'You *can't* get writer's block. You have to show up, and you might pitch 20 terrible ideas in a row, but it doesn't matter because maybe the 21st will be good. This reminds me of people learning a foreign language who say, "I don't speak it perfectly, so I'm afraid to speak." Well then, you'll never use that language. So as a writer, you have to be willing to suggest really bad ideas and hopefully be in an environment where you're not punished for that. One of the things I can do as a show runner sometimes is think of something that I know is bad but I'll pitch it anyway just so everyone feels, "Well, *he's* pitching bad stuff, so it's OK." I can model how not to be thin-skinned, that I don't expect that everything is going to be gold. In fact, 90 per cent of it is going to be crap. But by encouraging any idea and forwarding the conversation, sometimes someone will say, "OK, it's not quite that, but how about this?" and the team actually needed the initial spark of the bad idea to build a good one. Silence is not going to turn into anything. If you're only soliciting ideas without coaching the process, at some point the group says, "We know what we need to do but don't know how to get there by ourselves."' The leader's job is to inspire the group to overcome their fears and take those important first steps forward. 'The only way to teach people to be more creative is to teach them to look for other perspectives and points of view, and to do that you have to get them to expand their personal freedom.'[5]

4. Start with the obvious

Another trick Reich uses when the team is stuck is not to push for originality but to start with the obvious. He might say, 'Let's step back. What's the *most obvious* thing we could do?' Because you're often not thinking that. You're thinking, 'I want to do something really different, clever, reinvent the wheel.' If you presented someone with this concept, what would nine out of ten hack writers come up with? Sometimes there might be a reason it's obvious and then you can do things to make it feel fresh. But you're starting with the obvious because everything *has* been done. I often think, 'That's been done. I've seen that. I don't want to do it again.' But it's been done a million times for a reason. There's something satisfying about it. For example, there's always something satisfying about someone who has a secret and doesn't want to get caught. Some fundamental things like that just *work*. So I have to remind myself, "Don't shy away from that. Just do it, and do it well." People may have seen that story a million times, but they haven't seen it with *these* characters and this particular version of it. And the fact is that audiences aren't as sensitive to things being too familiar. I remember the *Grey's Anatomy* pilot and I asked myself, "Are they doing the thing where she sleeps with a guy and it turns out he's her boss?" Funny enough… yeah, they are! And 50 seasons later, it seems that was fine. So it's OK. Everyone borrows.'

5. Change feeling

Sometimes the solution is not to encourage a different answer but to spark a different mood or energy in the room. In Japanese gardens, if you walk from one area to the next, the garden might suddenly look and feel entirely different, which in Japanese is loosely translated as 'change feeling'. If you walked into the writers' room of *Friends*, often they would not look as if they were working. They'd be tossing a ball around, playing some stupid game, or just talking about something that seemed totally off subject. But very often they would do that for a while and then someone would ask, 'Wait a minute. Is there a story in this?' So often, just shooting the proverbial sh*t, appearing as if they were wasting time would lead to, 'Wait, there *is* something here!' The writing team would play all kinds of games in that room, such as 'What would this character do in this situation?', because everyone had to be able to write for every character. There were times when the room would just get really quiet. Everyone was stuck. So how do you get unstuck? Reich understood that sometimes the group just needed to blow off that steam, or be shocked awake, or laugh, or indeed just 'change feeling'. Often what can start that change is simply saying something outrageous and beginning a random conversation.

6. Change environment

If one level of unsticking a group is to change mood, then the next level of getting unstuck is to take a team into a completely different environment. Reich says, 'I've taken teams of about four people on a walk, going back to my earliest writing experiences, maybe not with *12* people because that becomes a parade rather than a walk, and you'd end up having a bunch of separate conversations. But after sitting for a long time and suddenly you're out in the fresh air and moving, that alone shakes things up. Or completely the opposite – a nap! I'm a big believer in napping for refreshing the brain. Sometimes you have to get out of the room when you're hitting a wall. It's also about keeping perspective to relieve the pressure I may be putting on myself. It's just a television show. Sometimes it starts to feel so weighty and serious, I have to step back and let go of whatever attachment of the moment I'm obsessing about. I also don't want to apply too much process in the writers' room, particularly early in the brainstorming or gestating of ideas. Structure comes later. First, we have an interesting idea or dilemma proposed. Then we ask how we fit that into a structure that makes it satisfying.'

7. Embrace the misery

Everyone thinks that getting unstuck is easier for everyone else than it is for them. Reich says, 'The fact is that it's misery for everyone. I try to be very open about the misery of writing. The more people that talk about that, the better. We may imagine that everyone's first drafts are just magical. No. Everyone's first drafts are terrible. But once you have a draft down, everything else gets easier. Just get it down, even if it's mortifying and you're thinking, "God, if anyone saw this, I'd be so humiliated." Doesn't matter – get it down! Then you'll look at it and inevitably see, "This isn't bad, and this is ok, and now I see how this fits" because you have this draft.'

That doesn't mean that to be creative you have to be some sort of miserable person. It just means that there can be a tremendous amount of angst in coming up with ideas. Inspiration is one of those things that you just have to trust. Working harder doesn't produce better results, but creating or recreating the conditions or environment for inspiration does. There is an urban myth that well-known TV writer and show runner Aaron Sorkin of hits like *The West Wing* takes five showers a day because he comes up with so many great ideas there. If you think, 'I *have* to think of a great idea for a show', it's not going to happen. The best ideas really often do suddenly appear, so Reich understands where all those mythical interpretations of genius come from, like a genie that visits you – a force outside of yourself. So how do you put yourself in a position to be receptive to those things? How do you relax, because it will never happen if you're looking at your phone and doom scrolling? Reich finds it may happen on a walk, being in nature, a beach, a forest, and of course in the shower. You do relax there to the point where you realize, 'I was clenching and working so hard, but as soon as I relaxed, *ding!* There's the solution.' You cannot 'hard work' yourself into creativity. Once you have an idea and an outline, then you can work hard. But at the inspiration point of the process, there's no forcing that. You simply have to trust the process, yourself and the environment that helps you get there. That might have to do with coming to terms with contrasts. As Bert Lahr, who played the Cowardly Lion in *The Wizard of Oz*,[6] acknowledged, maybe great comedy comes from making light of something that's dark, foreboding or seemingly hopeless, and great tragedy comes from losing something that's light.

Using pressure to your advantage

Writing for television has its own acute pressure with its demands to produce a quality episode every week. Taken at face value that deadline might seem only to constrict creativity, but Reich sees it differently: 'I don't know how you get anything done without a deadline because you can think about things and tinker with them endlessly, but a deadline is really clarifying. My personal creative process doesn't work without a lot of angst and misery that I have to go through. I'm not able, unfortunately, to be calm and confident. I usually have to sink pretty deep into a hole and just be so stressed about it that I will then come up with something. I hate that, but it seems I just have to accept it. For example, I'm working on something right now where I'm in a pit of despair, but I'm starting to see that I may come up with something. It's possible that the pit helps to spur on the creation in my process.' In other words, Reich embraces not only the pressure but the stress and hopelessness that he might not make the deadline, and that paradoxically enables him to work through it.

So first, the deadline helps you to force your idea out into the world. Second, you have to put on yourself the pressure of sharing your idea because you lose perspective after a while. You get too close to it, so you need that fresh pair of eyes and ears. Reich is a big believer in testing ideas in a relatively safe environment, when the stakes are lower, whenever possible. Putting this little bit of pressure on oneself earlier on in the process increases the odds of a successful pitch when the stakes are higher. Reich explains the concept in this manner: 'If there's a situation where you can present an idea for the first time, and the stakes aren't super high, where you aren't blowing an opportunity by presenting your idea at an earlier stage, then setting that deadline and doing that first pitch, even if it bombs, is good. At a certain point, you need to let the idea out into the world in some way. With what I'm working on now, I kind of knew on some subconscious level that this first pitch we did wasn't going to go that well, but we needed to do it because otherwise we'd just be stuck. I wouldn't have wanted to pitch it to a buyer, but because this was a preliminary stage, there were no real consequences other than it feels bad or you feel you let them down. So I thought, "OK, got that out of the way, it will definitely be better next time."'

Finding opportunities to test ideas when the stakes are low allows the creator a free pass to prod for weaknesses in the idea. There's *some* pressure because you are still being vulnerable sharing an idea, but putting yourself under that pressure is really a necessary thing for innovation which is *value-adding creativity*. As composer and conductor Leonard Bernstein once said, 'To achieve great things, two things are needed: a plan and not quite enough time.'[7]

Reich recalls an example of a *Friends* episode that was approaching the brink of disaster during production week, where the team used that pressure to make the episode one of their finest and Reich's personal favourite. It's titled 'The One Where Everyone Finds Out' (season five, episode fourteen) and is on everyone's top ten list. Until this episode, Chandler and Monica's relationship has been a secret to everyone except Joey. There's a game of sexual chicken between Chandler and Phoebe where Phoebe is trying to force Chandler to admit to his relationship with Monica by suggesting that Phoebe and Chandler sleep together. The table read went horribly. It wasn't working; it didn't even work the next day. Reich remembers, 'It was just one of those things where we were working unbelievably late at night. We worked a lot of really late nights on that show. It's hard to remember the specifics, but something cracked that episode open. I think it may have been this whole idea that "they don't know that we know that they know", and once we started building on that, there was this avalanche of flowing ideas. Today, when I watch the episode, it feels as if it must have always been written in stone, that we *must* have purposely written all these prior episodes in order to get to the payoff of *this* episode. But we didn't. We didn't know until *that week* that we were going to do it that way. Originally we thought Monica and Chandler were going to get together and break up after three or four episodes, and that was going to be it. *That* was our plan! Their relationship ended up lasting for the rest of the show's life, six seasons, because the audience reaction was huge. And we kept finding more fun with it, like this secret-keeping thing that we felt we could have fun with for an episode. As that was happening, we and the audience were getting more attached to this couple, so all our original plans went out the window. If we were rigid and said, "Nope, we've decided we're going to do it this way. We're not going to change," then that would have been a shame. It was important to have that ability to pivot, go in this new direction, and throw a lot of stuff out that we had planned because this dynamic was working.'

A lot of Reich's best memories of *Friends* are actually episodes like this where the table reads were absolute disasters: they're in production week, the table read's on Monday and shooting's on Friday! That pressure is immense, but sometimes you know deep down that you have to start from scratch on something you've been working on for months and were sure was going to work. It's not pleasant initially, and Reich remembers many days when he was still revising the first act at midnight. And it's exhausting, but then: 'There's something so satisfying about that crucible moment when we fix the problem. I think we maybe became a little addicted to that feeling after we had it, so that sometimes we'd do it when it wasn't completely necessary. Looking back, we might have created some crises where we threw out episodes that were probably fine.'

If pressure can sometimes be a spark for creativity, the leader may also ignite that spark by *inventing* pressure. That dynamic was displayed perfectly in an episode of *The West Wing* about a US presidential debate during election season. The seated president, Jed Bartlet, is about to go out on stage when Abigail, his wife, cuts off his tie with a pair of scissors! His team runs around to find another suitable tie and Jed storms onto the debate stage in a high state of energy *and focus* as a result. I'm not suggesting that you deface your team's wardrobe, and this technique of inventing crises will work better with some personalities than with others, but it's worth keeping in the toolkit when appropriate.

Arvind Ethan David

Arvind Ethan David remarks that he studied law at Oxford University 'for my sins'. A serial entertainment entrepreneur, David's first start-up was called hahabonk, which sold short-form animation to British broadcasters and helped launch the careers of scores of comedians. After earning his MBA at London Business School, integrating his creative and business experience, David founded Slingshot Productions, which was at the vanguard of producing micro-budget digital films, what we now simply call independent films. As an executive producer at Ideate Media, he produced and co-financed 76 episodes of television programming including two seasons of *Dirk Gently's Holistic Detective Agency* starring Elijah Wood and based on the Douglas Adams book of the same name.[8] In 2019, management bought the business from its investors and rebranded in the US as Prodigal Inc, which brings together all of David's passions under one roof.

David produced the Broadway musical *Jagged Little Pill*, based on the renowned album by Alanis Morissette, and both the film and musical versions of *The Infidel*. In the world of television, David writes for Neil Gaiman's *Anansi Boys* for Amazon and is adapting the Stoker-nominated comic series *Darkness Visible* for Intrepid Pictures. David's graphic novel, *Gray*, is a reimagined, modern, feminist take on Oscar Wilde's *The Picture of Dorian Gray*. He is a partner in Hatch Escapes, the escape room company behind *Lab Rat*, voted the top escape room in Los Angeles. With the team at Hatch, David co-created 'Mother of Frankenstein', a table-top 'escape room in a box' game inspired by the classic novel *Frankenstein*, which launched as a Kickstarter during lockdown. As if all that isn't enough, David is currently creating and will produce an immersive theatre production of Douglas Adams' *Hitchhiker's Guide to the Galaxy*[9] in the US. In short, David is a creative polymath. His career has been characterized by making things happen, both as a producer and as a creative himself, convening exciting and collaborative teams, not resting on his laurels, and challenging assumptions about the media and methods his company can tap into in order to entertain the public with new and relevant offers.

David is convinced that arts can enrich business. Similarly, he believes that those who are closest to innovation, to creating and selling offers to the customer, are those who are best equipped to lead the company. He reflects, 'I'm suspicious of companies that put the finance people in charge. The product and marketing people should drive, and by the way, they're usually the most creative colleagues in the company and so would help the organization's innovation culture. Put the people *with ideas* in charge.'

Despite his preference, and indeed necessity, for creativity at the forefront, David has learned not to innovate on too many fronts at the same time when it relates to the *type* of innovation on which he focuses. For example, the corporate executive might need to consider:

- product and service innovation: new offers or adaptations of existing products;

- process and technological innovation: re-engineering how something happens internally or installing a digital efficiency such as SAP;

- strategic innovation: questioning one's assumptions and rethinking the business model such as:
  - Who is your customer?
  - What do you offer your customer?
  - How do you offer it?

- platform innovation: creating an ecosystem that you manage or broker, such as iOS or Amazon Web Services;

- management innovation: adopting new models for how you recruit, organize, engage, incentivize and lead your people.

Any of these levels can be useful. The further down this list one goes in terms of where to innovate, the more one's competitive advantage becomes inimitable for one's competitors because copying or adapting near the bottom of the list takes longer, is more expensive or just messier. David advises not to do business model innovation at the same time as product innovation. As a guide on where to begin, he starts with the story. He is in the storytelling business after all.

David asks himself, 'What innovations do I need to consider as a leader in this company that will better serve this new story that I want to tell. Follow the story wherever it wants to go. The nature of "story" is hardwired into the human psyche,[10] so you must focus hard on the story and let that set all that follows: strategy, distribution, marketing, hiring. Steve Jobs knew the iPhone was about storytelling, for example.'[11] Let the product tell you what the strategy should be and find the processes and people that will allow you to do that. Creative projects are by definition not set from the beginning. They're start-ups or single-purpose companies, if you will.

An outsider might assume that Prodigal is all looseness and nothing formalized, but the company is rigorous in its processes. David is not against setting a conformity of approach where it serves. He asks himself with each project where he wants to introduce coordination and consistency and which areas require innovation: 'Clarity is useful when the physical product requires a degree of rigidity such as managing a store or adhering to the regulations of the musicians' union for rehearsals and performances. Slack is useful for most of the projects in our company. But we are legitimately detail-oriented about coordination and not creating small mistakes in execution because, for example, there could be big repercussions if we piss off a star because we did something stupid.'

David also wants consistency in his managerial roles at Prodigal since productions can fall apart when show runners change, for example. He notes, 'Great television has high cohesion among the writers, producers, directors and actors. The same is true with Disney executives, Disney Theatrical[12] and Pixar in particular. The Marvel universe has also enjoyed huge stability in its directors and actors. They enjoy a core group of collaborators.' In the creative industries, there is a long tradition of teams' forming, dissolving and forming again. At the same time, some companies attract some of the same key people who will join and re-join that organization from project to project. We typically don't find that anywhere else outside of start-ups or heavily project-based companies. In addition to desiring a group of consistent collaborators, David recognizes the need for a team to have a number of clear roles that people play in order to maximize innovation.

Team roles in the writers' room

In addition to considering how best to produce innovation in his company, Arvind David is intensely focused on each production or project team's dynamic so as to increase the odds of productive creative collaboration. In other words, maintaining the team's processes and practices is as important as their outputs. In the spring of 2022, a good deal of David's time was composed of leading the writing and creative team for his upcoming immersive theatre production of *Hitchhiker's Guide to the Galaxy*. I was fortunate to be able to observe four days of this team's meetings in order to note how David led and how the team managed their dynamic to maximize the creative quotient of their time together.[13] One of the most interesting dynamics to observe was the clear role that each person played in the conversation based on what was needed in that moment. While there are a number of team roles in all manner of practitioner frameworks and academic papers, here are the most useful roles in a creative context:

- devil's advocate;
- optimist;
- plant;
- customer;
- technical specialist;
- coordinator.

The devil's advocate

David set up the meetings on the first day with managing expectations about how he prefers challenge to automatic agreement, and that the team should expect that he would ask them to defend their ideas: 'I'm not a writer from a family of writers. I'm a writer from a family of lawyers, which means I only understand adversarial process. So I only believe an idea is good if someone's willing to fight for it. Please be relaxed about that, as you'll get the same back from me.' We heard a similar ethos from Andrew Reich, that ideas should be tested early and often so that you can work your way to good ideas, that the 'pitch' refines the idea (we also will hear this approach from Sir Clive Gillinson at Carnegie Hall in Chapter 5). At first, we might assume this approach contradicts the 'yes, and…' suggestion we explored earlier, but these two styles in fact work together. The trick is not to apply both simultaneously. Earlier on in developing an idea, 'yes, and…' is the more useful approach. As it refines and we start to see the realities of its implementation, then testing the idea's rigour is important.

The optimist

The role opposite the devil's advocate is that of the optimist. Because these *Hitchhiker's Guide* meetings that I observed were at the midway point, where a first script had been written but full production decisions hadn't yet been made, David encouraged a free flow of ideas. For example, a suggestion was made to ask the audience to hold hands and sing in order to save the planet before it's blown up. It's a typical Douglas Adams vibe to mix tragedy with comedy and cynicism. David nixed the idea but explained why and followed up immediately with encouragement to continue to throw out more ideas, playing devil's advocate in the first second and optimist in the next: 'I want actual pathos at this moment, but I'm glad you threw that out there. No idea is too goofy.'

The way in which David directed this conversation was very similar to how Andrew Reich described his role leading his own writers' room, that his writers need to propose 20 ideas, no matter how bad, because the 21st is likely to be a winner. A creative team always requires the optimist, believing that the next idea will be amazing regardless of what has come before.

The optimist is not only cheerleading ideas but building upon them, contributing the additional, hidden value that the team hasn't considered yet, or other directions where that idea could develop further. The optimist also integrates multiple ideas in addition to being the Zen master of 'yes, and...'. In the *Hitchhiker's Guide* meetings, the team was determining how they would tell the story of the character of Fenchurch rematerializing from Ford's memory of her (after she had died in the planet's destruction). One person suggested that when Arthur is strapped down to have his brain examined by alien mice (if you're overwhelmed by this absurdity, I'd recommend that you read *Hitchhiker's Guide to the Galaxy*), his memories of Fenchurch keep resurfacing. The director of the production, who is also a choreographer, suggested that different variations of Fenchurch could appear in a dance throughout the room. Then another person offered that these variations could integrate into one person, combining to recreate the comprehensive Fenchurch just as she was. Everyone loved the idea, and it's noteworthy that it took three people to get there. The solution did not emerge from just one individual (like Athena emerging fully formed from Zeus's head) but from the team all donning the optimist's hat to build on a promising idea.

The plant

The plant is the proposer of ideas, the creative wellspring in the team, the person who helps ideas to grow (hence 'the plant'). That doesn't mean that others can't or shouldn't throw out ideas, but the plant's explicit role is to be a font of original creativity. When their roles are explicit, the plant and the devil's advocate can enjoy fruitful and fascinating conversations. They are not in opposition to each other per se if they are both dedicated to surfacing the best possible idea and not settling for mediocre. In fact, they welcome each other's input. If these two people know their roles in advance of the meeting, the plant can prepare their ideas further in anticipation of the challenge they will receive from the devil's advocate. This practice improves the quality of ideas before the meeting even begins.

Sometimes the originator of the idea is not one person but two. We saw this with Andrew Reich's first stage of his career creating new television show ideas with his writing partner, Ted Cohen. A plant in a team can therefore be a pair. In the case of the *Hitchhiker's Guide* meetings, this pair was composed of the production's director and assistant director. They clearly had prepared their suggestions ahead of the meeting and therefore pitched their ideas more effectively with lots of 'yes, and…' to each other's comments and anticipating the pushbacks they might receive from the devil's advocate.

The customer

Whether designing for the experience economy (theatre, sports, amusement parks) or for fast-moving consumer goods (toothpaste, soda), it's useful for someone in the team to wear the hat of the customer, consumer or client. This prevents the team from digressing down a rabbit hole of what they find interesting, taking no notice of whether the concept will actually appeal to a paying customer. As with any team role, it's useful explicitly to announce what hat you're wearing to avoid confusion about what you're playing at or repetition from too many people wearing the same hat. David does this literally with his team and tells them when he's playing the role of an audience member: 'I'm taking off my technical hat and putting on my experience design hat. There's another character and that is the audience and what they're experiencing.' Reminding the team about the audience's perspective is particularly crucial given the nature of the immersive theatre experience they're designing, whereby the audience literally *is* another character with whom the cast interacts throughout.

The technical specialist

Sometimes there are more technical considerations that a pure 'ideas' team could not integrate into the conversation. A technical perspective might even be someone with experience in what the group is discussing so that this person can explain the challenges and solutions to implement. The *Hitchhiker's Guide* meetings included a line producer with deep experience in immersive theatre and technologies, which have their own challenges over those of a traditional live theatre production. When the team began asking how they would move the audience from room to room in a manner that didn't jar the audience out of their suspended disbelief, one of the technical specialists contributed, 'In immersions with simultaneous scenes happening in multiple rooms, there's often a sound or lighting cue that tells the cast and crews in the different rooms that they have to move their audiences on to new scenes.' This person had the credibility of their experience to back up the suggestion. A technical design solution was required in that moment, and if the team hadn't had that role present, considerable time could have been spent trying to solve the problem.

The coordinator

A team may require different roles to be played at different moments, and the same person can even play different roles at different times. As the team leader, David most often plays Belbin's Coordinator role, which is about maintaining or improving the overall team dynamic versus purely the output of the conversation. We heard this same message from Andrew Reich as he described his key function as the show runner. David makes his team maintenance role explicit in the conversation, particularly when he switches roles and gains permission to play that role.

In this chapter, we learned how two of our most preeminent creative minds solicit innovative ideas from their teams. From Andrew Reich, we saw how he would break his team into smaller groups when it became counterproductive to have a dozen writers working on the same task. But Reich's practice has primarily illustrated several novel approaches to crack one of the scariest creative challenges: how to get unstuck when the team has lost its spark. From Arvind Ethan David, we learned that consistency of approach or team can be a virtue, that creativity is not chaos. He also urges leaders of any level or industry not to attempt too many tiers of innovation simultaneously, such as trying to adapt one's business and management models at the same time. Finally, our observations of his creative team's collaborations on *Hitchhiker's Guide* illustrated the value of individuals playing clear roles that serve to enhance the team's dynamic, all ultimately in service of improving the quality of their creative outputs.

Any manager in any industry will be confronted with challenges and opportunities that require leading a brainstorming session to identify an unobvious solution. The technical skills to lead that session effectively are the very same skills and techniques that we have seen utilized in a writers' room or indeed in any creative team.

One thing you can do on Monday morning

Very early on in my experience teaching and consulting to creative companies, and then organizations in all industries, I identified a three-part structure to invent and explore new ideas within a team dynamic: ideate, evaluate, select. This structure does not imply that you accomplish everything in one conversation; it might require several.

The approach outlined below can be facilitated with groups as small as three and as large as 100. But this is a structure that has served me well, and you will see as you read on how this was practised implicitly in both Reich's and David's team meetings.

1. Ideate

Everyone proposes ideas. Nothing is shot down. You're going for quantity, not quality. So much research on creativity indicates that the best ideas emerge from many ideas, rather than one, proposed at the beginning. Ask the team to consider the answers to the 'exam question' well before you all meet in person. This will be helpful for the introverts in your team. Stress that you want a *lot* of ideas rather than each person to bring 'their best idea'. You don't want the team to edit itself, as the group itself can pull out value and explore the hidden depths in an idea more than the individual owner of the idea could. When you get together, ask everyone to say or write down (writing it all down on a wall is best) all their ideas without any feedback. Then ask, 'What else?' Ideas proposed may have sparked new ones that haven't yet been offered. Capture those topics too.

At this stage, think of yourself and your team as an oak tree. The oak wants to produce more little trees, but it doesn't know where the best combination of soil, moisture and sunlight will be. So its strategy is to drop thousands of acorns over as wide a space as possible. The tree maximizes its chances that some of those acorns will land on the perfect plot of land.

Yet most organizations when trying to produce new ideas behave more like pandas when they try to reproduce. With the encouragement of zoo keepers, a panda couple might attempt it once per year if they're lucky. It's such a rare occurrence that it becomes a global headline when a zoo announces a new baby panda. As a result of these divergent strategies from nature, we know that we have no shortage of oak trees in the world, while pandas are an endangered species. Here is the lesson: *be the oak tree, not the panda!*

2. Evaluate

Only when the team has a wheelbarrow full of ideas should it even begin to assess which ones to explore further. Only now do you formally close the 'ideate' stage and move to 'evaluate', when you now want people to respond to the proposed ideas. The team should all play the role of optimists first, and only when that stage is complete should the leader ask for devil's advocates. In other words, encourage people to first only 'yes, and…' the ideas, or at the very least nominate their favourite ideas and why. Try to solicit at least one 'yes, and…' for *every* idea. Only at the end of this stage should you ask the team why they may have concerns about some of the ideas, why they may not work, or why they don't excite.

As the leader, you should always contribute last in the 'evaluate' phase! If you state your opinion at this early stage, everyone else will assume that the decision has already been made. And if the leader judges every idea as soon as it's proposed, immediately playing devil's advocate, they will find in short order that no one pitches any more ideas. Before deciding to kill a proposition, it's also useful to consider the mood and energy of the room, as Andrew Reich discovered in his writers' rooms. In this way, the soil is fertilized for the next request for pitching new ideas, as everyone's egos have been protected. After this exercise, then one can reasonably decide a short list of the best concepts.

3. Select

Based on the previous stage, what ideas excite us most, have the biggest upside, the smallest downside, are the easiest to implement? Which ideas, though perhaps difficult to execute, would be worth the effort? You don't necessarily have to bring it down to the one idea and declare, 'OK. We're doing this!' The reality in corporate life is that you may have to run this by other people who are not in the room. However, you now have a lot of reasons, perspectives and additional contexts to contribute to those conversations as a result of the team's brainstorming. As Andrew Reich noted in his own role, the team leader needs the bigger-picture perspective in making the selection of which idea or ideas to pursue from the shortlist. Make sure the team knows the criteria in advance of the exercise and then apply those criteria with some rigour. In that manner, selection is not subjective, random or showing favouritism.

I cannot stress enough that regardless of the size of the group, you must devote adequate time to this exercise for at least five reasons. First, while you may reach the point where all ideas in the room are captured if you hurry, you will not have true buy-in from the group. Sure, everyone will have dutifully completed the exercises in the time allotted, but it will become about task completion rather than shared agreement that everyone can get behind these answers. Second, and related to this point, the meeting is not only about capturing ideas. You will require at least as much time to discuss which ideas the group will willingly advocate as the time you spent generating those ideas in the first place. Third, you need time to draw out multiple views. If you rush, the extroverted personalities and/or the most senior people in the room will jump in with their ideas and the introverts and junior colleagues will defer. Fourth, don't presume that silence implies assent – it might also mean that some people were not given adequate time or space to share their opinions or that they are not confident enough to speak up unprompted. Finally, and perhaps it goes without saying, the participants in this exercise should ideally include those with the authority and influence to align the company or department around the decisions made during the meeting(s), but these discussions should not solely involve these people.

Endnotes

1 Interview with Andrew Reich, 6 October 2020.

2 I was also a member of The Exit Players during my own time at Yale and directed the group for a year, but my time there did not overlap with Andrew's.

3 Ryan Bort, 'Behind the scenes details from "Secrets of the Force Awakens"', *Newsweek*, 14 March 2016, https://www. newsweek.com/star-wars-force-awakens-secrets-learned-sxsw-436787 (archived at https://perma.cc/J2WY-7T6D)

4 Meredith Belbin, 'The nine Belbin team roles', https://www.belbin.com/about/belbin-team-roles (archived at https://perma.cc/7R45-TLAV)

5 Arthur Gogatz and Reuben Mondejar, *Business Creativity: Breaking the Invisible Barriers* (Houndmills: Palgrave Macmillan, 2005), 131.

6 *The Wizard of Oz*, directed by Victor Fleming (Culver City, CA: Metro-Goldwyn-Mayer, 1939).

7 Classic FM, 'Leonard Bernstein quotes', https://www.classicfm.com/composers/bernstein-l/guides/leonard-bernstein-quotes/great-things/ (archived at https://perma.cc/PXW4-2PLM)

8 Douglas Adams, *Dirk Gently's Holistic Detective Agency* (London: Pan, New Ed., 2012).

9 Douglas Adams, *The Hitchhiker's Guide to the Galaxy* (London: Macmillan, Main Market Ed., 2009).

10 Lisa Cron, *Wired for Story* (Berkeley, CA: Ten Speed Press, 2012).

11 Interview with Arvind Ethan David, 2021.

12 Disney Theatrical produces Disney's stage shows.

13 Recording of writers' and creatives' team meetings for immersive theatre production of *The Hitchhiker's Guide to the Galaxy*, 1–4 March 2022.

05

Managing risk and leading adaptability

The realm of performing arts

In typical corporate life, we assume that the forming, familiarizing and normalizing of behaviours, eventually leading to high performance,[1] might take 6–12 months before a team is working together confidently. But in the world of theatre arts, casts, orchestras and crews must find their rhythm in a matter of days, and disperse and reform in new teams regularly, often several times a year.

I once directed a stage production of the Cole Porter musical *Kiss Me, Kate* for which we had 12 days to rehearse. You read that right. Not 12 weeks but 12 days to build the set, design and hang the lighting, rehearse the actors and orchestra, choreograph the dance numbers, practise the technical cues, and dress rehearse before opening night in front of a paying audience. Fast forward several years and I'm advising corporations on their team effectiveness. A consumer goods company leader confessed to me, 'I have a new team. We've only been working together for nine months, so we're really

not clicking yet.' I think I stared incredulously for a nanosec-
ond, thinking to myself, 'What is your team waiting for?
Divine inspiration?!' But I calmly replied, 'Well, let's talk
about how we can get them firing on all cylinders in just a
few days.'

Let's take one example of how this promise might be
drawn out. What is happening in the theatre that isn't
happening in the boardroom? It turns out that a number of
habits, assumptions and conversations occur in the theatre
world that are indeed distinct. For example, there is more
focus on the process – *how* we will work together – and from
that attention one may tease out the details of good habits.
We know from the discipline of organizational behaviour
that a new team forms more quickly the faster its members
can build empathy for one another. One empathy-building
exercise that I used as a director (my first career) with a new
cast was to present the team with a physical, cooperative
challenge. It could be anything, such as building a pre-defined
structure like a castle with blocks as quickly as possible.
Each person would explain without interruption how they
proposed to build it and what, from their experience and
background, led that individual to use that approach and the
role they would play in its construction.

As the leader of the team, I ask questions to draw out
stories from that person's life as they speak. The group discusses how they will achieve the objective, integrating several
of the perspectives shared, then tackles the challenge.
Regardless of how they perform, the cast has taken a step
forward in terms of thinking of themselves working together
as a more integrated group instead of one driven by a single
expert, or even just by me as their director. In asking each
person to be explicit about the role they would play, I'm

also pivoting their perspective towards the maintenance of the team (the how) rather than only delivering a successful performance (the what or the result).

As it turns out, there is very little happening in the playhouse that represents a prohibitive or impossible habit that a traditional company can't practise in the warehouse. It would be wrong to assume that a theatre company is not thinking about thriving financially, and indeed the most inspiring and creative companies unsurprisingly are usually the most profitable. When we flip to the corporate boardroom, how much time does the typical leader spend to enhance their people's creative capacity every day?

Let us identify, therefore, the mindsets, habits and exercises practised by creative professionals, including Jeremy Sturt, Creative Director of consultancies Lively Arts and Just Add Water in London, and Sir Clive Gillinson, Managing and Artistic Director of Carnegie Hall in New York City. We also must answer the critical question: 'How can these techniques transfer to corporate life?' Luckily, we can also find examples of pioneering organizations outside of the arts that regularly dedicate time and effort to enhancing adaptability and inspiration to produce innovative outputs and better results.

Lively Arts and Just Add Water

Creative agencies Lively Arts and Just Add Water provide the perfect case study for this chapter. They use techniques from the theatrical arts to foster creativity, collaboration and unity with their clients from many different industries.

When London West End stage manager and producer Jeremy Sturt was working at Imagination Entertainment

25 years ago, he was helping the company to be a bridge between the arts and the corporate worlds with regard to creative intellectual property and to be a challenger brand in the world of live performance. The company produced large-scale events such as the Big Picnic in Glasgow, an immersive, interactive piece of theatre. Sturt was thinking about moving on from Imagination, and one evening one of the company directors said, 'Look, there's a guy named David out there who's talking to McKinsey about something but has to work out how to produce it. You should go and have a conversation with him.' So Sturt went along and met with David. His idea had been shortlisted to one of five that McKinsey wanted to try out for a workstream at their annual partners' conference in 1995.

That year, the workstream was owned by the McKinsey London office to create and run this piece. The client at McKinsey was London's managing partner, Norman Sanson, who tasked a couple of his team members to consider how to boost the firm's creativity and innovation, how those qualities would be valued, how important they were for the business, and what the necessary characteristics would be to enable creativity and innovation to thrive. Their broad understanding was, 'Let's go to the arts and see what they have to offer.' They had come up with these various ideas and David, being an opera singer, said, 'I think we should try to get them to do an opera!' His idea was to work with McKinsey's global partners and their significant others to write, design and perform an opera at their annual retreat in Portugal at a critical time in the firm's life under new leadership and with the recognition that they had to enhance their collaborative and innovative culture.

What made that idea compelling, and swung the decision their way, was the level of interaction and engagement proposed. David and Sturt bottomed out the idea and approach, presented it to Sanson and he said, 'Yes! I love the idea. You're on point for delivery.' Sturt answered, 'Great. I'm used to that as a producer. I'm in the business of putting on theatre.' There was the right mix of David as a performer and Sturt as a producer, which made the important difference and ensured that the idea could realistically be executed well.

Implementation included building an amphitheatre for 400 people from scratch in the grounds of what was then the Sheraton Algarve hotel. Sturt and David took six trucks and 50 or so 'theatre luvvies' – technicians, propmakers, wardrobe assistants, lighting designers, riggers, storytellers, script writers, actors, musicians, four theatre directors and four choreographers – to collaborate with three cohorts of 400 McKinsey partners and their significant others. The partners had no idea what to expect. When they arrived in their hotel rooms, they found two feathers and a note on their pillow telling them to arrive at the amphitheatre at nine o'clock the next morning after breakfast. They dutifully turned up and saw a short performance created to explain what constitutes putting on a piece of theatre (i.e. the musicians played, the singers sang, the storytellers told a tale, everything was linked to a story). When that finished David announced that they would perform in three days' time after undertaking a series of rehearsals, interventions and different workshops with the team.

They went off into four big groups doing immersive, interactive improv and storytelling work, and then each person had choices to make. They could stay in their big storytelling group, which would compose and perform one of the four main chapters of the opera, or they could choose a discipline such as lighting, wardrobe, prop making, music. Over the next three days, they completed a series of workshops and rehearsals to allow people to engage in interactive theatre but also to build a story. Their story, which they could interpret however they wanted, was structured around *The Conference of the Birds*, a poem by Attar of Nishapur from the 12th century,[2] about the birds of the world flocking together to select a new leader and undertaking a journey of strength before realizing the true leader is within, a neat metaphor for an organization exploring its future.

On that final evening, each cohort performed their opera, a well-received denouement, where the whole conference came together, followed by a wonderful celebration. But actually, the real learning was what happened through the whole process of the workshops and the partners' engagement. Those workshops were the measures of success or failure much more than the final performance. They created an event which lived long in the memory, but the run-up to that was extraordinary in how it embedded ways of thinking and what one can do to exercise one's creativity.

The three-day conference ran three times, on each occasion stripping down the amphitheatre to a skeleton and then reimagining the opera with each new group, really challenging the directors, scenic designers and choreographers to help the delegates come up with fresh ideas so that it was truly the McKinsey partners' story. Afterwards, it had quite a radical effect on a number of individuals in terms of resetting their ways of thinking around how they create, what they innovate with, what's possible and how they engage. In a few cases, it reset their relationships with their loved ones. Some spouses reported that their partners were more talkative at home, singing in the shower, more present and happier.

The McKinsey story illustrates that there is also an intangible value in what the arts bring. There's an infectious richness there which governments typically have lost sight of and don't often support. That intangible value was certainly one of the takeaways many McKinsey partners and spouses remarked upon which they had never realized before: that you could get so many diverse cultures together and create something so special. It was all about and by 'us', not someone else putting on the show.

David and Sturt created their business doing work like the McKinsey engagement almost immediately after the conference. They called it Lively Arts. Over six years the company grew a reputation for creating an innovative approach to bringing the arts into business. It wasn't a skills exchange, it was really about, 'Tell us your purpose, your values, the story that you're trying to get across, and we will co-create innovative ways to address that with your organization, and indeed with other stakeholders, drawing from our theatrical background.' People loved it. It was the nineties, a lot was changing in the character of how business happened, and clients craved an experience that was radically different from what they'd been used to.

One of the most prominent Lively Arts projects concerned employee engagement work around the formation of the company Diageo, which was a merger between Guinness Brewery and Grand Metropolitan. These organizations were two tribes with two huge head offices that didn't want to come together. There were a lot of early office conversations like, 'Hey, that's my desk!' because they had been intense rivals for so long. So the situation sanctioned by the CEO required disrupting their fixed mindsets with some simple theatre work. Lively Arts took a trio of actors who were dressed as if they worked in the office, whose job was to show that life was not the same: 'This is not your screen, your desk, your potted plant. This is a brave new world. We're going to be disrupted with transformation.'

One actor dressed as a maintenance engineer would stop people in the hallway and ask them to help him carry a rolled rug to the other side of the building; he used that opportunity to get them to open up about what excited them about their new corporate environment as they unrolled the rug and physically changed the environment at the same time. There was a 'cleaner' with a large feather duster whose job was to pop up unexpectedly and get people to laugh and recognize that their new world could be fun and surprising. Of course, positively disrupting one's work environment to consider what's new and changing doesn't always require hiring a troupe of actors. White goods company Bosch approached this opportunity in its own way.

Bosch

We know intuitively that our work environment easily hinders or promotes creativity, collaboration and adaptability in our work practice, and influences whether our perspective is drawn inwards or outwards. Dr Birgit Thoben, the international innovation manager of corporate research at Bosch, applied a similar approach to that of Jeremy Sturt among her research and development team in order to spark their creativity and expand their perspective of the possible. Growing up, Thoben had wanted to study the arts, but her parents persuaded her to choose the more 'sensible' career of engineering. But Thoben never lost her passion for creativity, which ultimately served her well in her career.

She said, 'When I became innovation manager at Bosch, my predecessor gave me the most valuable of presents: a huge empty space, which eventually became known as Platform 12, in which I could create something completely new, anything I wanted, as long as it would be beneficial for innovation.'[3] The purpose of Platform 12 was to encourage the Bosch engineers to come up with new ideas and build prototypes. Thoben decided to invite an artist to work in Platform 12 and act as a kind of catalyst. She did not give the artist exact instructions on what to do, nor did she tell her colleagues who he was or why he was there, only to shake things up to make the engineers think and question. As with the Lively Arts' actors disrupting routines at Diageo, this artist built sculptures, but he also slept in a tent during the lunch break and drew on the windows. He did everything he could to provoke the Bosch employees and spark conversations among them.

After a while, disruption surrendered to collaboration and the engineers organically began to work with the artist, which resulted in new ideas, technologies, processes and perspectives. Despite these rewards, many colleagues told Thoben that she was crazy and that her approach would never work. Yet many years and many ideas and inventions later, Platform 12 remains. As Thoben said: 'Platform 12 helped Bosch transition from a very traditional culture to a much more open-minded and innovation-driven approach. Self-reflection grew across the entire company, people asking themselves deeper questions like, "Does this legacy process actually make sense?" It really changed their behaviour and their mindset. The artists helped them ask questions that they never would have thought of asking before.'

Thoben's approach is growing in popularity, in fact, as the bold examples of art-related projects at Nokia Bell Labs[4] or Google have proven. In these times where the lines between industries are blurring, cognitive diversity in innovation is more important than ever and we will see these types of cross-industry, cross-talent and cross-skills collaborations only increase. Some of the results: words that appear out of white tapestries, music that streams out of fabric, a mysterious blue cloth-draped spiral that guides you with light and sound. It may sound like a fantasy novel, but these are real works of art made possible with Jacquard,[5] part of Google Advanced Technology & Projects and Google Arts & Culture.[6] Combining advanced hardware and software technology with textile and manufacturing know-how, Jacquard helps designers make digital experiences out of everyday objects. An ordinary denim jacket[7] or a rucksack[8] transforms into something that answers calls, plays music and takes photos. In March 2019, Jacquard created an artists-in-residency programme to bring together technology, art and fashion. It is a unique opportunity for creative communities to enhance their work digitally – by weaving Jacquard technology into physical installations – while remaining focused on the original design.[9] This is a commercial application emerging from a process similar to that of Bosch's Platform 12, creating novel products springing from a rich mix of diverse perspectives, particularly from whisking together engineering and art.

Back to theatre

Lively Arts wasn't finished with Diageo after the introduction of pop-up artists-in-residence. They had more radical, theatrical experiences in store. Sturt and David created a metaphorical event, where they transformed London's Old Vic Theatre into a huge, bowl-like play area. As hundreds of Diageo employees arrived from both of the former companies, they were directed to different doors, walking through tunnels into a bare space in the middle of the theatre, with a huge wall of cardboard boxes down the centre. Deliberately, no one else was there, so people were standing around asking, 'What am I meant to do?' Eventually one of the employees took down one of the boxes and sat on it. Then someone else did the same thing and finally everyone was seated on the boxes across this whole area. That was the cue for Diageo's CEO to come on stage and say, 'Great! You passed test one. This is all about breaking down barriers, and we're going to spend a whole day exploring how we can creatively break down the barriers among us. Let's be very clear: we need to engage with these new values and new ways of working and that's what today is all about.'

In groups, they discussed and wrote their future story and came back into plenary and performed their stories of Diageo moving forward. There was both interactive silliness and great fun, but at the same time there was focus on the core context and story of the business. The next 'act' involved a game in which an actor dressed as Elvis emerged, singing 'Are You Lonesome Tonight?' while six blindfolded Diageo colleagues were each presented with one element of a Burger King meal in front of them (Diageo owned Burger King at the time). They had to find one another and assemble a whole meal for Elvis, so that he would stop singing. Silly stuff, but it firmly reinforced the new Diageo values; everything was rooted in the work of the business. If that didn't happen, they would just be putting on a show to no effect.

Since that event went very well, Lively Arts were next asked to work more closely with Guinness, which was struggling to take on board the new Diageo values.[10] The brewery had previously had its own brand values, which were far more resonant because of Guinness's long heritage. The objective of this new engagement was to recognize that brand values are important but so are the core values of Diageo, and Guinness employees hadn't yet considered how to live and breathe those. Diageo's young, enlightened CEO, Stephen Nelson, who later went on to run Heathrow Airport, emphasized, 'We have to live the values, live the strategy, and enable everyone in the organization to understand the importance of those.'

To achieve this vision, Lively Arts took about 1,500 Guinness people and a theatrical troupe of about 50 to a film studio in Hertfordshire. Nelson took the stage and said, 'We're going to focus on the values today, but we're going to do it in a different way.' Employees were divided into 'tribes' and a metaphorical story was presented that every 100 years the tribes of this universe come together to compete in a theatrical Olympics. Each tribe had its own Guinness value to represent, but they were going to be refereed on the basis that: all the values had to be experienced in the work they presented back. A core team of directors and choreographers worked with each group to perform their piece for their colleagues. The finale was the realization that all the tribes won because they all effectively lived and breathed the values. So it wasn't ultimately about competition but about unity. The day culminated in a huge celebration.

The event embedded the importance of both living the values and understanding one's purpose in an organization. But once again that was accomplished using metaphor, theatre and story. The team succeeded because they interrogated the client beforehand to understand what they actually did, then ensured they had all the necessary theatrical skillsets to brief the participants well on the day within that clear context of the organization.

Growth mindset

This technique that Lively Arts applied at Diageo is one experiential way to shift individual perspectives from a fixed to a growth mindset. Such a shift is incredibly important if an organization has any hope of collectively embracing a new normal, which by definition requires the willingness to let go of the old. Professor Carol Dweck of Stanford University has researched growth mindsets extensively and her research points to the growth mindset as the foundation for all organizational change.

The company that is plagued by a fixed mindset has a tough road to travel in any transformation journey. In such firms, you will hear managers lament that 'people don't want to change' or 'change is frightening'. The organization's frames are the preponderance of its community's individual perceptions. To diagnose, therefore, whether an organization suffers from a fixed mindset, a useful approach is to ask its role models, its leaders, how they perceive change, experimentation, volatility and ambiguity. That will give you a fairly accurate snapshot of the character of the whole corporation because individuals will consciously or unconsciously observe those people who are successful in a company and emulate their language and behaviours.

The table below contains the phrases we hear in a fixed mindset company versus a growth mindset organization, whose leaders and role models sing a very different tune when it comes to trying new things, embracing change, taking on board feedback, and being willing to fail, learn and grow. Any change agent needs to pay close attention to the language they hear and to celebrate that their job has become much easier if typical phrases include those on the righthand side of the table.

Fixed mindset	Growth mindset
Failure is the limit of my abilities.	Failure is an opportunity to grow.
I'm either good at something or I'm not.	I can learn to do anything I want.
I don't like to be challenged.	Challenges help me grow.
Either I can do it or I can't.	My effort and attitude determine my abilities.
Feedback is personal.	Feedback is constructive.
I stick to what I know.	I like to try new things.

I'm sure you can see at this point why a growth mindset is foundational to any change initiative – it is a measure of the organization's capacity to both contemplate transformation positively and implement that transformation with confidence. To try, learn, adjust and forge on is dramatically different from an aversion to any attempt that doesn't achieve 100 per cent success. Ironically, many companies think they are mitigating risk by studying, planning, pitching and earning multiple levels of approval in various committees before a finger is lifted (months or years later) in relation to actual change. The quest for perfection in this case impedes any progress.

Such a hypercautious approach ironically assumes much greater risk. Think, for example, of what it costs to launch a new grocery item into national distribution. According to Nielsen, the market research firm, of the thousands of grocery products that are launched each year, only 25 per cent will be on the shelves a year later.[11] This suggests that 75 per cent of the industry's new product spending is wasted. And remember, we're not talking about a 75 per cent failure rate for small, low-cost experiments here but a 75 per cent failure rate that includes high-profile, heavily funded, national rollouts. The culprit? A lack of experimentation both before and after launch. Therefore, we need to make fewer big bets and a lot more smaller bets at the individual and team levels, and all that starts with the attitude of a growth mindset.

Storytelling

After six years with Lively Arts, Jeremy Sturt formed Just Add Water with his business partner, Claire Sampson, which to this day helps companies transform using theatrical, experiential techniques.[12] The company's contention remains that theatre and an arts-based approach more broadly are incredibly effective at engaging and moving teams at pace. Sturt and Sampson knew with more certainty with every passing project that this approach works despite its radical novelty, that it can have a profound effect and that it's not as risky as one may initially assume. It allows organizations to reflect on their narrative, the story that they're actually trying to express internally or externally.

Companies usually buy that this narrative of where a company has been and where it's going is a story that must be set within a context. Theatre, through using narrative and storytelling, can be a powerful tool to set context really quickly. An illustrative, purely theatrical, example is the musical *Miss Saigon*. The narrative is a simple love story at its heart, but the wider context of the Vietnam war is massive and it gives the play its epic sweep and engages the audience. There are also clear, archetypal protagonists: you have a jilted lover, two people who should never be together but are drawn to each other, and the clever commentator-critic. The McKinsey 'Conference of the Birds' and the Guinness Olympics had that epic sweep. In both cases, the organization was put front and centre, the participants were the protagonists or heroes at the heart of the whole piece, and they created a simple narrative with a cast of characters around it. Those characters were the companies' colleagues themselves, so they could see themselves and tell their story within their own context. All the elements of a strong story were there, which made engagement quicker and more powerful:

- epic sweep;
- narrative;
- the protagonists' tale with their backstory.

If you have those components, if people can immediately see themselves in the story and you take them along with speed and enthusiasm using professionals they trust, even though they're immersed in a world they haven't experienced before, then they are in a state where they can consider and practise transformation. An observer would have witnessed an epic tale, but the genuine magic was happening on a much more personal, micro-level through each participant contributing to the performance. That's when change happens – when the individual can understand their role in their organization's new story amidst this larger context of their world, region, industry or market. Executives talk about how their people need a sense of purpose, and that's true, but at its heart you first need their engagement to pursue that story for themselves.

Carnegie Hall

Sir Clive Gillinson is the executive and artistic director of the iconic Carnegie Hall in New York. From 1984 to 2005, before moving to the United States, Gillinson was the managing director of the London Symphony Orchestra (LSO), having been called to leadership from the cello section in which he had played for 14 years.

While I met Gillinson 18 years before our interview for this book, I was eager to speak with him again, as I rarely meet someone holding both creative and commercial leadership roles at the same time.[13] Almost every theatre I've encountered was led by an artistic director and a managing director – two distinct roles held by two people with distinct backgrounds. I asked Gillinson if his two roles ever found themselves in opposition or if they always complemented each other. He spoke at length about how he always found his experience to be helpful: 'I take more risks this way. It enables me to be more entrepreneurial. I have to behave like the founder of a start-up. I would never do a job today that didn't encompass both because the fascination is both developing ideas that are as extraordinary as we can possibly conceive and then working out how to fulfil them. My instinct, and I may be wrong, is that leaders probably take more risks with this model because, having been involved in developing the ideas, you then kill yourself to find ways to make sure they can happen. Whereas if I were just the managing director and somebody else came up with the ideas, I would probably be more cautious about what we might or might not be able to do. Because I'm centrally involved in the development of the ideas and passionate about them, and absolutely certain we have to do them, I then have to take responsibility for making them happen. That means I'm going to be more demanding on the organization in terms of what risks we should take and how we make sure that we also mitigate risk as much as possible, whilst ensuring we make the best possible things happen. It certainly makes the greatest possible demands on your entrepreneurial spirit. It ensures that you're demanding the absolute maximum, both of yourself and of your team.'

Gillinson sees his role as closest to a Steve Jobs or Jeff Bezos: Jobs was instrumental in developing Apple's projects, but then he also had to make sure they could come to fulfilment. We read about these founder-entrepreneurs and know they are at the cutting edge of where their companies are going, but they are also taking full responsibility for making sure projects happen and that they're sustainable. Gillinson muses, 'I would guess that leaders who wear the creative and commercial hats simultaneously are much more common than we think. My view is that any leader has to behave as if their organization is a start-up, not an established business, in terms of risk and in terms of how you challenge yourself.'

Preparation and connection

In his early career as a cellist at the LSO, Gillinson already understood some conditions under which his leaders, in this context the conductors, would draw out connection, mutual understanding and creative flow from their orchestras. One element was how the conductor led rehearsals, ideally using the preparation to build up to a peak performance. Some did this well and others did not, even among the most accomplished. Gillinson's comparisons raise fascinating reflections for business leaders on preparation and connection with their teams: 'There's something very puzzling about the skill of a conductor. There was one conductor who always did the most brilliant rehearsals. He was really inspiring. You got extraordinary insight into the music. You knew exactly what he wanted and he had a fantastic conducting technique as well. And then you arrived at the concert and nothing extra happened. The performance was just like a first-class rehearsal.'

Gillinson contrasts this conductor with someone like Claudio Abbado, one of the greatest conductors with whom he ever worked. However, Gillinson found rehearsals were boring because Abbado said almost nothing except 'Louder, softer, quicker, slower' yet communicated little about his analysis of the music to the players. Gillinson recollects, 'And yet, come the performance, it was just unbelievable because Abbado could communicate in every way through what he did then. He had a phenomenal technique. He could express everything through how he conducted: through his eyes, through his expressions, through his movements and so on. Truly astonishing! We all knew exactly what he wanted even though he'd virtually not said a word in rehearsal. Come the performance, we knew what to do and how to play as he wanted it. These were some of the greatest performances any of us ever did, but the rehearsals were not enjoyable.'

Gillinson remembers an even more baffling conductor who had hopeless technique. He couldn't conduct well but had an extraordinary, magnetic personality and astonishing understanding of the music. All the way through his rehearsals, musicians would be coming to Gillinson, who was in management by this time, to say, 'We can't work with him again. This is hopeless. He really can't conduct.' But after the performance, they'd all be turning to Gillinson and saying, 'When's he coming again?' because the performances were unbelievable, better than those from many top-quality conductors. On the face of it, these three conductors could not have been more different in the experience of the orchestras they led, but they all succeeded in their own right.

Some leaders of the orchestra just did not rise to the occasion and seize the frisson of energy that comes from performance when it matters most. Gillinson recalls there was one conductor with whom rehearsals would be fascinating. He was utterly brilliant, he could do anything, but he often almost played with the music rather than led it: 'Because he could do anything, he seemed to want to show you he could do anything, like a conjurer, but that's not about communicating something profound or insightful about the music.'

The paragon of conductors for Gillinson was Leonard Bernstein, who in Gillinson's opinion had everything. He relates with relish: 'Bernstein was probably the greatest conductor I ever worked with both in my time as a player and as a manager. His rehearsals were fascinating, with astonishing conducting technique and insights into the music, the composer, the context for the music and more, and then the performances rose to an even higher level. He could do all the communication verbally as well as physically when he was conducting.'

One of his great friends and admirers said of Bernstein, 'The thing about Lenny is he always lives at the edge of risk, and he's somebody who, if he falls off a ladder, will never fall off the bottom rung. He'll fall off the top.'[14] Composer Stephen Sondheim said that Bernstein taught him 'the only chances worth taking are big ones'.[15] The fact is, not every Bernstein performance was an extraordinary performance because sometimes he went over the top, was overindulgent, and it didn't work. But most of his performances were among the greatest experiences any who worked with him can remember.

This survey of conductors makes a very important point about leadership – our organizations require leaders and not just experts. Leading this social construct that we call a 'company' is less about technical expertise and more about a distinct portfolio of leadership skills and capabilities, including strategic thinking, communicating and executing, and exciting others to exceptional performance.[16] A leader can garner respect in the acknowledgement that they are excellent at the functional expertise with which they rose through the ranks, but it is their ability to lead that the enterprise craves and which provides a complementary role to the experts in the organization. In addition, the leader must distinguish between when they are leading others versus managing issues, how they lead versus what they lead, such as the conductor 'toggling' between leading musicians and managing the performance of a piece of music. But note that it's never about garishly displaying, peacock-like, their own ability. The leader's skills are complementary, leading others and leading issues, opportunities and innovations, and making sure the right questions are asked and the important conversations take place.[17]

Leadership principles

Over his many years leading organizations that rely on creative production, Gillinson has formed his own leadership principles, which act as touchstones that govern his decision making, priorities and management:

1 *Never be satisfied. 'Good' does not really matter; only be interested in the extraordinary*. No idea and no output are perfect at first. Always try to improve an idea, performance or format. If you had a brilliant season, the next one can't be 'more of the same'. It must be even better and offer artists, styles and formats that are different. You have to push the boundaries all the time.

2 *Questions are more important than answers*. You have richer conversations that contribute more insight if you start from the perspective of curiosity rather than expertise.

3 *You must always take risks, push yourself and your audience*. Feeling safe is dangerous, as that is the creativity killer. You always have to seek and take risk, but you then have to manage that risk in the best possible way.

4 *Don't offer something to the market unless you're convinced the world can't live without it*. This principle means that every idea must be world-class and possess some aspect that is unique and obvious in its appeal to a wide audience. The lens Gillinson uses with his people is, 'We've got to work on this project until it's reached a

point where we think the world can't live without it. That's got to be what you feel about it, that it *has* to exist. And if it *has* to exist, the chances of your being able to convince other people to partner with you in making it happen are very high.'

5 *Give your people space.* Gillinson is adamant that he should not micromanage his senior team. At the same time, he wants to ensure that his vision and priorities are aligned with those of his team. So when a new member joins his executive team, he stays closer to them for a while until he's confident that this leader understands what Gillinson would wish them to do and understands the culture and values of the organization. Then he gives them a lot of room to be entrepreneurial and take ownership for their department's success.

Let's take a deeper dive into a couple of these principles.

You must always take risks

Organizations usually take a view that to innovate is to take more risks and so risk and creativity are conflated. Gillinson argues that this isn't necessarily a bad thing, but you have to possess the right perspective about holding these two conditions in balance: 'You can't run anything successfully without taking risks. My view is that the greatest risk of all is trying to avoid risk because then you're almost guaranteed to fail. So I'm an absolute believer in taking risks. I'm not interested unless we're taking risks. We have got to be breaking new ground all the time, trying out new things. But the most crucial thing to me is not about taking a risk, which is fundamental, it's how you manage risk.'

Gillinson admits that he started out by taking risks which were probably unacceptable. When he moved from being a cellist in the LSO one day to being manager of the orchestra the next, he heard that the conductor, cellist and one of the greatest artists who ever lived, Mstislav Rostropovich, was going to celebrate his sixtieth birthday with two orchestras. Gillinson went to Rostropovich's manager and said, 'This is crazy. Why is he doing this with two orchestras? It should be *one* orchestra so there's a singular focus on him.' She said, 'Well, it's such a massive project that each orchestra can't afford it on its own.' So Gillinson put forward the offer for the LSO to do it solo. The manager said, 'But you're on the verge of bankruptcy', and the LSO *was* on the verge of bankruptcy when Gillinson became the interim manager. That was the only reason he went into management in the first place (the previous managing director had lost his job as a result). But Gillinson retorted, 'That's the way it's got to be done for Rostropovich. It's such an extraordinary project for one of the world's greatest artists, I'm sure we'll find the money.' At that, the manager went to Rostropovich and told him about this lunatic at the LSO and what he'd said, and Rostropovich responded, 'Well, if he believes in me like that, I believe in him. And if he's a cellist as well, then that settles it!' Rostropovich brought the project to the LSO, they *did* raise the money, and they were better off financially and artistically for having taken the risk.

Gillinson admits, 'The fact is at that time I did not know how to calculate risk, so it was purely based on my view that this project had to happen in that way, and if I believed it then I could get other people to believe it. But that was, I would say, an unacceptable risk. When I went to the board and declared, "We'll raise the money", they said, "Are you sure you can raise it?" I said yes, but obviously I had no idea except my conviction that it had to happen. Nowadays we would never do that. But my view about projects is, firstly, I'm not interested in *good* ideas: they have to be *great* ideas because who are you ever going to excite about just a good idea and why are they going to give you money? It's got to be extraordinary.'

Today, unlike the Rostropovich example, Gillinson will work out the strategy with his team for how the organization will implement the idea and how to raise money for it, but at the end of the day there is still risk. No matter how much you're convinced yourself, you still have to convince other people. At the same time, Gillinson can't remember a situation where he couldn't persuade others to back an idea if he and his team were convinced in the first place that the idea was amazing.

For example, creating the National Youth Orchestra of America was a huge demand, and Carnegie Hall decided on the level of risk they were willing to take before embarking on the project in earnest. They decided that if they could get a few founder patrons to donate $1 million each over five years (because they felt it couldn't be launched with just one year's funding, it had to be five years at the very least), then they'd have the possibility of underpinning the project with long-term funding. The team thought this was going to cost something like $10 million over five years. If a critical mass of founder patrons could be found who would give sufficient backing so that everybody believed it had to happen and would happen, then they'd raise the rest of the money. And that's exactly what they did: Carnegie Hall succeeded in getting three or four founder patrons at $1 million each and that was sufficient to provide the launchpad.

Gillinson recollects, 'If we were able to get several people to put in a million as founder donors, that tells you about the importance of our idea. I mean, that's a lot of money to commit! You would never be able to sell it if you haven't got a great idea. There wouldn't be a hope in hell. The fact is, by going out and saying we've got to raise three or four founder patrons, we were effectively checking risk because it meant that if nobody had come in, we would have known it wasn't a compelling enough idea and we wouldn't have gone with it. If nobody had given anything, you have to listen to that. So that was how we approached that project – you eliminate some of the risk and you calculate the rest of the risk.'

Once you have those platform advocates, it's simpler to attract other supporters because they see that the idea has already been vetted. After that stage, it's much easier to raise money for something that exists. As Gillinson elucidates, 'The minute the National Youth Orchestra play and people can hear what it is, and they can hear how extraordinary it is, it's much easier to be inspired about giving money than people selling you an idea, where you have to believe it when they say, "This is going to be one of the greatest National Youth Orchestras in the world. It'll be a phenomenal orchestra with huge impact in terms of international understanding as they travel the world as youth ambassadors for their country." The theory is always less powerful than the fact. The minute it exists, it's much more fundable.'

Gillinson set Carnegie Hall a target: they would only go public with the National Youth Orchestra and put it on the launchpad if they had raised $3–4 million of the $10 million they required to fund the first five years. Thereafter, they'd still be raising money, but by that time they would be flying with commitments around a real project rather than a concept. If the worst came to worst after two or three years, it was possible that Carnegie might have had to scrap the Youth Orchestra if they couldn't raise any more money. But the initial risk related to the fact that they knew that once the orchestra had performed, people would be blown away by it and that would draw in the rest of the money – and that is precisely what happened. Gillinson recalls, 'We definitely didn't raise the full five years of funding before the orchestra played. You've got to try your very best to create a position where you're not taking 100 per cent risk. We'd eliminated 30–50 per cent of the risk before we started, whereas I hadn't eliminated any of the risk at the LSO with the Rostropovich decision.'

Gillinson is really speaking about the power of displaying a prototype rather than merely summoning an image of what an idea could be. This practice is core to Pixar Animation Studios' success with its ever-present habit to 'Display'.[18] If you are walking through the Studios, you can't help but encounter work-in-progress, whether it's an open screening of the dailies of a film, or a gallery of character studies or storyboard drawings. These displays serve as an instant visual representation of the state of play, inviting everyone, even those just walking by, to contribute. Thinking of work as being in a state of perpetual Beta and inviting comments, questions and improvements facilitates learning, widens ownership of the challenge and ultimately leads to better outputs. All told, Pixar will often produce 12,000 storyboard drawings to make one 90-minute feature film.[19] The company wholeheartedly buys into the power of prototyping.

Danish toy company LEGO is also a fanatical proponent of prototyping and getting as many colleagues as possible to offer feedback. Former LEGO brand manager for southern

Europe, Per Enggrob Larsen, recalls, 'We would invite people from all markets to give feedback on concepts. We'd be looking five years into the future and thinking about which way the market will go. We'd look at loads of drawings and knock down this huge pipeline to about 25 concepts. They we'd go to year three and what will launch then. We'd see prototypes and sample product boxes. We would give feedback on these concepts all the way from five years from launch down to a product launching in 12 months where we would delve into detailed discussions about box sizes, pricing and volume.'[20] In this manner, LEGO reduced the new product pipeline risk by applying all the market heads to comment on possible launches, refining their thinking each year on each product from five years out to one.

Gillinson remembers another aspect of eliminating risk was not only attracting donors at the beginning but attracting world-famous artists to collaborate: 'I knew that, in a country the size of America, the standard of the students would be among the greatest in the world. But I also knew we had to get a great conductor for the National Youth Orchestra at the beginning. That would also de-risk the project. I managed to get Valery Gergiev, and Gergiev bought it sight unseen because he believed in Carnegie Hall, and this is where having a brand has huge power. But you have to have such a compelling idea, and you're pitching it at a level that's right because without a great conductor, we wouldn't have gotten concerts and television in Moscow, St Petersburg and the Proms in London. Without Gergiev, we wouldn't have gotten Joshua Bell, one of the world's great violin soloists. So all the pieces have to interact with one another, and if you go for a safer approach, if we'd gone for a conductor who wasn't one of the world's superstars, none of the other pieces would have fallen into place. You've got to go for broke on every single part of implementation. I knew we had to get the international concerts and television, but we also had to communicate that Carnegie Hall was an institution that will only do things if they're extraordinary. With all our projects, we set out to create a magnet for talent, so all the parts work together to ensure that every element is world class.'

Once a company has the reputation for 'going for broke' on absolute quality with every offer to the market, there is a shift in the customer–supplier relationship whereby market research to a large extent is disintermediated by the trust in the supplier. In other words, the customer trusts that a new product or service is worthwhile because they trust the source of the offer. Without the permission to invent things the world doesn't know it needs, a company can never reach tomorrow. Market research only tells you about what already exists or what the world already knows.

Gillinson recognizes this truth: 'Steve Jobs sold things that market research would have told him he couldn't sell. But Jobs' view was always, "I've got to create something that people want, but they don't know they want it until I've created it." That was exactly the same with the Walkman at Sony. Sony did all the market research around the Walkman, which told them it wouldn't work. Japanese companies were not necessarily known at the time to be huge risk-takers. Sony chairman Akio Morita was, however, and he said, "I know it will work. We're doing it. Never mind the market research." He believed in it, and of course it was an extraordinary success.'

Returning to the medium of theatre, the actor may have one audition from 20–50 submissions and earn one job from every 20–50 auditions. Over a short time, the successful actor learns quickly that to win more work, they have to achieve 'cut through' to stand out. To do that *requires* taking risks. They have to innovate and consider how the other 50 actors at the audition would *not* interpret the scene they're reading. The casting director then sees something fresh and memorable. Even if the choices that actor makes are not quite correct, most casting directors are more likely to think, 'Well, they're willing to take risks and make interesting choices. We can always give them direction to focus the performance.' So achieving creative cut-through isn't simply about out-grafting everyone else. That's a mistake that has been deeply embedded in the Western concept of success: 'Much of the capitalist world was forged under the influence of the Protestant work ethic, a philosophy that holds that enjoyment and leisure are sinful, and that only through austere work activities can people prove their true worth. This world view produces characters who shun all pleasant impulses and activities that might generate joviality (Oliver Cromwell banned Christmas as Lord Protector of England; the United States' forefathers came from this branch of Protestantism) in favour of long work hours and personal thrift. It produces a culture that celebrates intensity, competition and doggedness.'[21] However, when new ideas seem ever harder to come by, bravery to invent, rather than just more effort, is more likely to produce a novel result: 'Cruising in third gear just maintains the status quo. If you want to get somewhere else, it requires the courage to push yourself into fourth gear, to risk seeing and trying new things. *It does not mean* just working harder.'[22]

Carnegie Hall faced perhaps the greatest challenge of its existence when the world entered lockdown amidst Covid-19. The Hall's survival depended on pivoting for a time to digital-only. For a live performance venue, this pivot required taking risks, in fact some of the most radical rethinking and reinvention that Carnegie Hall had ever attempted. With its education programmes, Carnegie Hall prior to Covid was reaching about 800,000 people a year, most of whom were children. All those programmes went virtual very successfully. Carnegie Hall also engaged with concert audiences by creating offers such as 'Live with Carnegie Hall', which was broadcast every two weeks, engaging great artists telling stories from their homes. Gillinson remarks that these were not significant financial risks, but they did involve a huge amount of staff time. His choice was, 'Do we get rid of a lot more staff or do we develop programmes that are really meaningful and that enable us to remain connected to our audiences?' He and his team made that decision first, as they were absolutely clear that Carnegie Hall had to stay connected with its audiences. Carnegie Hall couldn't disappear for what might be a year or longer.

Gillinson told a patron about all the things the Hall was trying to do in transitioning to virtual and he earned a donation specifically to do that. But in order to change the way Carnegie Hall worked, the Hall had to go to a lot of prior donors as well to say, 'The programme you're funding will no longer exist physically for the time being. You've given us funding that is designated for us to spend in a certain way. Are you willing to adapt the criteria of your funding so that we can do these other things to ensure that we can address our mission virtually until live events return?' Almost everybody gave Carnegie Hall the freedom of movement in these extraordinary circumstances.

The second argument Gillinson made to acquire financing in order to pivot to digital was that Carnegie had an opportunity to reach a much broader, global base unshackled from trying to reach people physically. So there were advantages because their reach was suddenly much more extensive and growing. But again, Gillinson had to build faith in his investors that Carnegie Hall could continue to grow even in lockdown, including major projects with significant risk and finances involved.

In this state of lockdown, Gillinson and his team were not only reacting to the global environment but continuing to invent the future, still executing and adapting what was in the Hall's pipeline of programmes: 'What's important is that you know what activities and projects really matter and that have to continue to exist. We looked at all our programmes, reduced the costs and reconfigured how they'd work so that they would not cost as much money. We worked out ways where we could still deliver on our objectives just as powerfully, which then means that when we focused on digital as a parallel or complementary dimension, we could really grow that. We wanted to ensure that everything that we did digitally would have meaning and validity once we were again back in person and that it would be complementary to what Carnegie Hall is about. Thus, despite the hardships of the pandemic, I think we've now become a much better organization, contributing much more to people's lives because the digital dimension remains and will continue to grow and complement the live element that is now largely back in full. I don't think any of this will replace what happens in the concert hall, which is a truly extraordinary and meaningful experience, and you'll never replace that digitally. But on the other hand, the reality is that probably 99 per cent of the world's population will never have the chance to visit Carnegie Hall because most of them aren't able to travel here. So if we can create a way to serve people who cannot have the physical experience but can have a digital experience, which is still meaningful and very powerful, then that again complements what we're doing. It doesn't take away from it.' Carnegie Hall truly turned the existential threat of Covid-19 into an opportunity to serve new audiences. They thought beyond surviving for several months and instead considered how to provide experiences to a much wider population and for an indefinite duration.

One initiative that Gillinson remembers in particular that had to adapt involved Carnegie Hall's national youth ensembles. They had already recruited 200 musicians who were going to play in those ensembles in the summer of 2020, but obviously they couldn't do that physically anymore. Carnegie Hall's education team instead put together a fantastic two weeks of digital learning and experiences, creating a fascinating and important community. Gillinson admits that this was not the same as working together face to face, but a lot of important value came out of it. After those two weeks, the education team asked, 'In the next year to year and a half, we'll all be together physically, but what can we do now using the learning of this year to make sure we can pass on the skills and experiences to a lot of other people who would never get into the National Youth Orchestra or National Youth Jazz and for whom we can't give the live experience?' So Carnegie Hall developed another series of virtual programmes for people who were not in the youth ensembles but to whom Carnegie Hall could nonetheless offer support, skills, knowledge and experience. Gillinson is particularly proud of the resilience that his team showed by staying focused on their audience and artists: 'That's just an example of how our team created many things which hadn't existed before that replaced what was lost physically but which had a life of their own going forward.'

To achieve radical creativity requires questioning how much we are controlling ourselves and our teams in terms of what is acceptable novelty. Are the boundaries we set as leaders too tight? Exponential creativity perhaps means managing less. Highly 'manageable' creativity will most likely at best earn incremental improvements rather than revolutionary ones. Recall our survey through history in Chapter 1, where we observe that whenever human society genuinely changed, the catalyst was a revolution when assumptions were overturned. The result was dramatic progress and invention. As author and educator Richard Farson concluded with his characteristically radical candour: 'Real creativity, the kind that is responsible for breakthroughs... always violates the rules.... In most organizations, when we say we desire creativity, we really mean manageable creativity. We don't mean raw, dynamic, radical creativity that requires us to change.... The problem with creativity in a lot of companies (and a lot of individuals as well) is that they just don't want to go through all the necessary changes. They want creativity the easy way. Manageable creativity means lukewarm, half-ass creativity, which unfortunately usually means no creativity at all.'[23]

Give your people space

Gillinson's view is always to give people the space they've earned but never give them all that space to begin with. Whenever a new person arrives, Gillinson initially stays very close to what they're doing until they've earned the space. He always says to his people, 'I never want surprises. If you think or know there's a problem, tell me as soon as it arises. Don't tell me only after our possible options are very limited or gone.' Gillinson wants an open culture where everybody will speak immediately if there's a problem. He is clear on this point: 'If you say empowerment is just letting everyone run free, it absolutely is not. And I expect my senior staff to do the same with their staff. I want to see them empower their staff, but equally, everyone should earn their space.'

Gillinson has seen leaders who never want to empower anybody and prefer to make all the decisions. When somebody thinks they know everything, they cannot keep the best people in their team. For Gillinson, avoiding this requires humility: 'I just don't know as much about each particular element of our business as all my senior team do. The head of marketing obviously knows more about marketing than I do, and the head of IT, etc – you can go all the way around. They obviously all know more about their particular areas, so if I'm not actually allowing their wisdom and experience, I'm limiting our potential. That is fundamental, but there's no point unless you appoint the best. At the same time, I don't ever want people who just want to run alone. I remember having a head of development/fundraising at the LSO who wanted everything to be her success. It was hopeless because she didn't want to give other people space to succeed, so she had to go in the end. This whole thing about empowerment has to be part of the culture of the organization as well as appointing the best people.'

How long is a leader effective?

It's amazing to Gillinson how many people say, 'I think the time limit to do a leadership job well is seven to ten years.'

Gillinson's view about all jobs is that if you don't feel you're contributing at least as much if not more than you ever did, you should be leaving anyway, but he managed the LSO for 21 years and still had many more things he wanted to do. Gillinson reflects that he can understand if somebody says, 'After seven years, I have no more ideas.' Then of course they should leave, but in such cases they shouldn't have waited until they had no more ideas – they should have known before that. But he enthuses that, after 17 years at Carnegie Hall, he feels more thrilled about what the Hall is doing and about all the possibilities than ever. In fact, he signed a new five-year contract in 2019 which will take his tenure at Carnegie Hall to 20 years.

Gillinson emphasizes that the 'acceptable' time in a leadership role is never about drawing lines arbitrarily around particular periods of time. When students come to see him to talk about their careers and say, 'I've mapped out my career. I want to do three years here, five years there', Gillinson always responds, 'You have made a fundamental mistake because none of us knows what we want to do. You *cannot* know. The biggest thing is to follow your talent, follow the things that inspire you and excite you, and always keep an open mind. Never think you know where you're going. By definition, that will limit your potential.' Gillinson always cites himself on this topic. As a cellist, the last thing he was ever interested in doing was going into management. He thought it was probably the most boring thing in the world. He wanted to be an artist and believed that was what being creative was all about. Moving into management wasn't the plan, yet he says it's the most creative thing that's ever happened in his life, and what's more, he's more creative every day than he ever was as a cellist, particularly playing in an orchestra where what you do is largely defined by the conductor.

In other words, if Gillinson had been certain that he didn't want to go into management and had kept a fixed mindset about that, everything that has happened to him in the past 35 years would not have happened – it has been the best time in his life. When Gillinson is asked to deliver commencement speeches, he always returns to this theme of growth mindset, keeping an open mind and following your talent and enthusiasms. In these addresses, he wonders aloud how many of those professors sitting on the platform are doing exactly what they set out to do in life and asks them to raise their hands if they're doing just that right now. Almost nobody raises their hand; that's the fact, and it is an immensely important one.

In this chapter, we've explored how using techniques from the performing arts can inspire new perspectives and shock people out of complacency or resistance to change, even in organizations as traditional (and perhaps as cynical) as McKinsey. Companies often cite their diversity as a competitive advantage yet frequently do not inject that diversity at critical moments with artistic collaborations and all their new ways of thinking that this can imply. We learned how leaders, such as great conductors, must invest as much energy in the research and preparation of new projects as they do in leading their people in the execution or performance of those initiatives. Successful leaders hold seemingly competitive dynamics in a creative tension: innovation and risk, freedom and constraint, prototype and fully realized project, spontaneity and planning. The trick is not to choose one over the other.

One thing you can do on Monday morning

I was struck with how often the concept of growth mindset occurred in my interviews for this chapter. Growth mindset assumes a tolerance for failure, which is too often anathema in corporate life. We know intuitively, however, that without failure, we're unlikely ever to experience dramatic success. And if we don't share failure, our colleagues are more likely to make the same mistakes. There are no knowledge economies here!

To shift a team's attitude towards embracing failure requires fostering an environment of vulnerability, where colleagues are comfortable, eager even, to share their learning from every experiment they attempt. One way to do this is for the leader to host a failure party. I hear you guffaw, but hear me out. One of the many reasons that Pixar's mantra is always to 'Display' is to invite critique, sharing and building on ideas. A failure party is simply to celebrate that spirit of Display. As psychological safety grows, colleagues become more comfortable to push the boundaries of what they think is possible, knowing that their personal reputation does not depend on inauthentically trying to communicate an aura of omniscience.

In the failure party, each person in the team who has explored a new avenue, experimented with a hypothesis, tested a prototype or interviewed a stakeholder or customer, and it did not go to plan, would share their activity, the result and, most importantly, the learning. Colleagues may ask questions, can build on the ideas and even pursue avenues that the speaker did not. The one thing that no one must do is belittle or criticize the speaker. Each dialogue ends with the conversation, 'what we learned here'. Some leaders of failure parties even toast every speaker when they finish with a ritual, be it ringing a bell or everyone shouting 'Huzzah!'. The speaker's candour, vulnerability and creativity are acknowledged. The 'party' element, which can simply involve refreshments and an informal environment, is proposed in order to put people at ease as quickly as possible.

The failure party is also a tremendous opportunity for the leader to share directly and obliquely what the boundaries of acceptable risk are. Over time, the team understands explicitly and implicitly what they can try right away and what they need to share first before trying. This dynamic is not unlike how Sir Clive Gillinson launched the National Youth Orchestra. Share the idea first, socialize it among donors to test the idea, get a bit of investment to display the prototype, then that generates further investment and ultimately produces a sustainable new programme for the world. The initial hurdle involves little risk, and once shared and improved, the idea proceeds to the next hurdle, with the team possessing more confidence that their concept has passed muster each time. At each hurdle, if the idea cannot pass further, then risk is controlled, lessons are shared and the entire team has still acquired greater wisdom.

Endnotes

1 Judith Stein, 'Using the stages of team development', MIT Human Resources, https://hr.mit.edu/learning-topics/teams/articles/stages-development (archived at https://perma.cc/97C3-TRRU)

2   Farid Attar (1984) *The Conference of the Birds*, Penguin Classics, London.

3   Laurence Van Eelegem, 'How an artist-in-residence program helped turn around a traditional company's innovation mindset and culture', nexxworks, January 23 2020.

4   https://www.bell-labs.com/programs/experiments-art-and-technology/ (archived at https://perma.cc/TFX9-ZQGW)

5   https://atap.google.com/jacquard/ (archived at https://perma.cc/UK52-2YNS)

6   https://artsandculture.google.com/u/0/ (archived at https://perma.cc/AR2Q-YNDB)

7   https://atap.google.com/jacquard/collaborations/levi-trucker/ (archived at https://perma.cc/5TW3-D5NR)

8   https://atap.google.com/jacquard/collaborations/ysl (archived at https://perma.cc/XH8W-SZEC)

9   Pamela Golbin, Google ATAP Blog, 16 October 2019, https://www.blog.google/products/atap/jacquard-and-google-arts-and-culture-weave-tech-art/ (archived at https://perma.cc/B6ZV-RHSZ)

10   Diageo's values are: Passionate about customers and consumers, freedom to succeed, proud of what we do, be the best, valuing each other.

11   Lara O'Reilly, '3 in 4 FMCG launches fail within a year', *Marketing Week*, 9 September 2014.

12   The author worked for Just Add Water from 2006 to 2008.

13   Arvind Ethan David, whose story we explore later, is another.

14   Interview with Sir Clive Gillinson, 2021.

15   Richard Woodward, 'The other Odd Couple', *The Wall Street Journal*, 3 December 2010.

16   Rob Goffee and Gareth Jones, *Why Should Anyone Be Led by You?* (Boston: Harvard Business Review Press, 2006).

17   Robert Kaiser, 'The best leaders are versatile ones', *Harvard Business Review*, 2 March 2020, https://hbr.org/2020/03/the-best-leaders-are-versatile-ones (archived at https://perma.cc/Y6XM-TDYY)

18 Helen O'Hara, 'The secret of Pixar's success', *Empire*, 19 July 2010, https://www.empireonline.com/movies/features/secret-pixars-success/ (archived at https://perma.cc/AQ73-VQBB)

19 Ed Catmull, *Creativity, Inc.* (London: Transworld Publishers, 2014).

20 Interview with Per Enggrob Larsen, 22 February 2021.

21 Barbara Fredrickson, *Positivity* (Oxford: Oneworld, 2009).

22 Arthur Gogatz and Reuben Mondejar, *Business Creativity: Breaking the Invisible Barriers* (Houndmills: Palgrave Macmillan, 2005).

23 Richard Farson, *Management of the Absurd* (New York: Simon & Schuster, 1997), 131.

06

Layered leadership

The realm of Imagineering

One of the trickiest elements of managing the process of innovation and adaptability, including large-scale corporate transformation, lies in managing the trade-offs between sociability (or how we get along) and creative tension, constantly pulling the team out of its comfort zone, encouraging debate and challenge. In this chapter, we will extrapolate lessons from the worlds of Imagineering (Disney's theme park and experience design) and Ellipsis, London's immersive, multi-media entertainment company.

Human first

Disney develops the creative muscles of its colleagues, all called 'cast members', by continuously moving them into new departments and roles. These placements are not decided based on 'best person for the job' but on 'what does this person require next in their development?'. With such rotations under their belt, an engineer for a Disney theme park, for example, would better understand the visitor experience for a new ride that they are tasked to design if they worked for a time with the creative team that prototypes new attractions. A guest experience is a synthesis of technologies, character or movie-driven stimuli, theatre, psychology, art and effective creative collaboration. Every participant in that process serves the team more powerfully if they are attuned to the influences and disciplines of every other team member.

Former Disney executive Dave Crawford studied mechanical engineering at UCLA. He knew from a young age that this was what he wanted to study, but he could not envision how he would apply his training. Ultimately, Crawford led the mechanical design and engineering team that builds the rides and attractions in Disney's theme parks around the world. This group is very aptly named – they are the Imagineers.

At university, Crawford thrived with his studies, but he wasn't *thrilled*; it didn't excite him every day. On a whim, and to add novelty to his week, he enrolled in a class in movie special effects and makeup. It was at this moment that he thought about how or if he could merge his various passions and skills into a career. While he was first exploring cinematic special effects, the emergence of Pixar Animation Studios was at the time disrupting the industry with the wide potential of digital. Crawford could see that more and more special effects were going to be delegated to digital graphic designers. With the help of an influential mentor, he shifted his attention from motion pictures to theme parks and rides, those feats of creative inspiration and mechanical engineering which are monuments to reliability, durability and safety. When he graduated, Crawford took a job with a small southern California-based special effects company that contracted to theatres and theme parks around the world to build concepts into reality.

Before long, Crawford saw that if he wanted to keep doing this on a bigger scale, the only logical company was Disney Imagineering. He joined the mechanical engineering department that conceived, designed and built ride systems for Disney parks globally. But Disney is very wise in how it builds cognitive diversity in its workforce. Crawford reasons, 'For true innovation, you can't just have a tolerance for risk. You have to create environments of creative friction where new ideas can emerge, and diversity enables that.' He happily could have stayed in his engineering lane, but the company moved him for five years to the Blue Sky team within Imagineering. This is the group that thinks up the park, attraction, entertainment and ride concepts in the first place. After all, if his career was to lead technical support and feasibility of new ideas, it stood to reason that he should learn how those ideas come to life in the first place. Crawford describes the experience as the most challenging and rewarding of his career to date: 'It was all possibility, exploration and creative friction.'[1] How many of us can describe our own work experience in those terms?

Crawford then spent seven years at the Research and Development group, the technical epicentre at Disney Imagineering, where he was put in charge of the team responsible for applying new technologies such as magnetic propulsion systems to rides and experiences. This role provided a masterclass in creating and manifesting new ideas that must withstand the test of time. After all, some Disney rides, such as Space Mountain, have not only endured but thrived for almost 50 years! Like Sir Clive Gillinson, Crawford understands that to have enduring creative ideas, one must straddle the commercial, technical and artistic worlds. He passionately preaches that this is absolutely possible and even essential within his field of engineering: 'There's a default assumption that writing or painting is creative but not technology or engineering. Engineering is *very* creative. It explores the new and useful versus what is just random. Engineering's ultimate goal is to improve human existence.' This technical–human approach not only applies to the role of the team, in Crawford's eyes, but it applied to his own function as a leader within Imagineering. One could argue that keeping the human consideration in synergy with the technical and commercial considerations is the most effective approach for a leader in any industry or function.

As a 'technical humanist', Crawford's leadership principles required to succeed in this high-wire managerial act can be summarized as:

1 Retaining the human perspective is critical – unconditional caring.

2 Make things real as soon as possible.

3 Optimism and enthusiasm.

We will explore these principles in detail one by one.

1. Retaining the human perspective is critical – unconditional caring

In other words, it's not just about giving assignments to individuals in one's team and monitoring their progress. Each project in Crawford's team lasted three to five years(!) and therefore he felt personally responsible for understanding each team member's career path. His criteria were not only

'I have to give this assignment to someone who's available', but 'Whose career objectives would best be met if they received this project?'. Crawford spent a considerable portion of his time every month in one-to-one meetings with his team members, asking questions such as, 'Are you fulfilled and happy? Are you encouraged that you're on the right path? Am I and Imagineering developing you in the right manner and direction for that path?' Crawford suggests, 'I have to have the true belief that my team's advancement is more important than my own.' He admits it can be exhausting, but it's also personally rewarding: 'I help people achieve their best. When I took on a role in senior leadership, I was frustrated at first because I didn't see the value I was adding on a daily basis. But the longer you're in the role, the more you see the impact your actions have on a team, department and organization. It's a marathon, not a sprint. Engineering is about solving technical puzzles, but I see a connection now in solving puzzles that enable people to be successful. For example, I may want to send a colleague to China on a project, but will his family tolerate that?'

A humanistic approach is congruent with Imagineering's purpose as well. A Disney experience is emotional and participative, so it makes sense that its leaders also step into participation – being open and close to their people versus managing from a distance. Imagineering's creative executive Joe Rohde says the organization is 'all about emotion. Humans are emotional beings, so you have to access emotion. That's what runs this thing.... You have to let yourself feel emotion in order to do this work.'[2]

Imagineering's focus on humanity is not unique to arts or creative companies. The technology company Panasonic recently revised its assessment process by which it identifies high-potentials from a gladiatorial 'thumbs-up, thumbs-down' approach after a gruelling assessment centre, where applicants have to undergo role-plays in excruciatingly tough scenarios, to a development approach that acknowledges the human beings involved in the process. Nominees now have opportunities to work on areas identified from the centre over several months, have the chance to improve, and are also given a six-month 'hot house' period to create proposals and pitches for new initiatives aimed on improvement within the company, even if those themes are outside their departments or functions. Amazingly, 50 per cent of these proposals are adopted and integrated into business as usual in the company. Managers too feel a stronger sense of mentorship for their charges who make these proactive contributions.

Panasonic's European Talent Director Wilsey Mockett has seen a massive difference where colleagues leave the development centre with gratitude instead of dread and are willing to propose new ideas simply because they are encouraged to do so rather than to 'stay in your lane'. She says, 'We don't need to deepen divisions in the organization. Amidst this talent shortage, we want people to be their best, to be great leaders for the future, and we need to encourage them to be so. That's a pivot toward humanizing our talent management.'[3]

2. Make things real as soon as possible

Show your work to colleagues so you all get on the same page. As we have explored earlier in the book, display and prototype! If you only describe, rather than show, your project, your peers will interpret your words in different ways. For example, at the time of our interview, Crawford's team was working on 'stunt-tronics', which was their term for animatronic stunts, or as Crawford described as bluntly as possible, 'How can you throw robots into the air?' A goal so conceptual with so many theoretical possibilities can only be realized and accelerated through testing if the engineers create many and varied prototypes and share them with their colleagues for feedback. The ultimate answer, not yet known at the time of writing, may very well be a hybrid of several solutions that the team tests at prototype stage.

Prototyping doesn't end at the first concept either. The prototypes just get better with more investment once they are approved. For example, Imagineering developed a ride based on an idea of hurtling through the Seven Dwarves' mine in a mining car, from the film *Snow White and the Seven Dwarves*.[4] The team experimented with the movement of the ride not only to be based on the direction of the track but with the car itself swinging with the kinetic momentum of the twists and turns. The team had to manage both technical risk, i.e. 'Will it break?', and what Crawford calls 'creative risk'. What he means by this is that a very reasonable question to ask at this stage is, 'Sure, it's possible, but is it *enjoyable*?' To be blunt, 'Will the swinging just make guests sick?' The only way to know is to test it! So once the mechanics of the ride were developed through early prototypes, the team built a mock-up of a couple of mining cars, enlisted groups of brave volunteers from among their colleagues, and drove them around an empty parking lot for two weeks so the riders could experience the suggestion of the ride's motion plus the additional dynamic of the cars' swinging at the same time. Prototyping is a common theme that I hear in most creative industries. If you can't see and experience it, you'll never know whether it's worthy of further development.

Optimism and enthusiasm

Management guru Tom Peters said, 'The leader is a cheer-leader.'[5] Within Imagineering, as in any research and devel-opment department in any industry, people come up with ideas, seek permission to spend time on them, fund them or both. The trick is to accept or reject the idea with positivity regardless. Not every idea is going to get the green light. After all, sometimes there really are bad ideas! But if the reaction from the leader is so disheartening, what are the chances that the direct report will come back to that leader with any other idea but a safe, bland, incremental one? So the leader has three crucial tasks at this stage.

First, redraw the line between sensible and stupid ideas. Don't make your cut-off point so conservative that you'd never consider ideas that were heretofore unknown but potentially worthy of exploration. Yes, Imagineering is a business, so that reality must be held in tension with the artistic freewheeling that sparks and grows enduring partici-pative experiences. Joe Rohde says, 'Imagineering as a place is very, very frustrating for business-minded people because several core characteristics of creativity itself do not recon-cile themselves with efficiency-based business theory. So there is a permanent tension. It's a question of keeping it in balance. That means you have to accept that it will neither be some kind of wild jungle of creative monkeys nor is it going to run like some kind of dystopian military facility. It's not going to be those. It's going to be this thing that's held in bal-ance between the two.'[6] Rohde's argument is that creativity naturally sits in conflict with conformity and the familiar, tried and true, and so the leader's job is to keep both dynam-ics functioning simultaneously. This is not new in academic literature, but many managers have not internalized the lesson in practice. Part of the explanation has to do with the industrial revolution-era paradigm that the leader's job is to manage conformity in and variance out, which by definition is antithetical to dramatic innovation. Richard Farson in *Management of the Absurd* writes, 'Real creativity, the kind that is responsible for breakthrough changes in our society, always violates the rules. That is why it is so unmanageable.... We don't mean raw, dynamic, radical creativity that requires us to change.'[7]

Second, if an idea is approved, give your team a lot of runway to pursue the idea in their own manner. When George Lucas challenged his team to overcome technical obstacles when making the *Star Wars* series of films, he simply invited them to 'think about it'. Almost every creative leader I've interviewed rejects micromanagement as a good use of their time, and more importantly understands that their team's quality and quantity of ideas would suffer if they did so. Crawford goes even further. While he's heard of the adage that the leader just has to explain the 'boundaries of the sandbox' and then the team can innovate within that frame, he says, 'Yeah, I'm not a fan of boundaries! I would rather give myself permission to think *outside* the box.'

Third, if you are rejecting an idea, do so with positivity and enthusiasm. Explain why the idea isn't a good use of time and, if possible, consider whether there is a different take or lens on the idea that could be explored instead. As critical as the idea itself, the leader must nurture an environment where people feel not only safe but enthused to raise novel concepts and designs. Crawford stresses, 'You must give that permission to explore again and again. You have to allow curiosity. It's one of Imagineering's defining characteristics. Yes, it can be challenging, but a lot of organizations don't encourage curiosity at all, and that's a problem. A command-and-control management style means that the leader only gets what they can imagine.'

One aspect of Crawford's character that you can never miss when speaking with him is his humanity. Every theme he discusses returns to the need to be empathetic towards one's team. To nurture creativity, that most human of qualities, one must be attuned to the humanity of the people with whom one works. Crawford brings all of his technical education and experience to his roles, but his leadership ultimately is impactful because he recognizes that he is managing people first and projects second.

Leading across different dimensions, or layers, is a common approach that I observe among managers who care deeply about the creative competency and outputs of their organizations. We shouldn't assume that to succeed at this 'layered leadership' is dependent on a given function or even on the personality of the leader. It is a skill and is worth investigating further with another example from the experience economy.

Layered leadership

If someone had gifted you tickets to what you thought might be a play called *Somnai* in London in 2018, you would have turned up to the address to find yourself at a warehouse down an alleyway. At this point, suspecting you may have been pranked, you might still be brave enough to crack open the nondescript door and stick your head through tentatively. A person inside would usher you into a pod, where you'd watch a short video explaining that you are about to enter your dreams. You're measured for a virtual reality headset, and you and a small group of guests drift through a series of rooms, each representing different dreams. Sometimes you're telling stories with an actor. Sometimes you're in a nightmare, working your way out of a child's room to escape a mysterious figure in a black raincoat. Sometimes, through your VR headset, you are flying in 'V' formation with a flock of geese over a spectacular landscape. As you rise in your harness, you feel wind blowing on your face. You would swear you're flying! What is this experience? It's primal, vulnerable, totally immersive, confusing, provocative, thrilling, and this just might be the future of in-person premium entertainment. One of the pioneers in this field,[8] the creator of Somnai, is the company Ellipsis. Its co-founder and CEO is Andrew McGuinness.

McGuinness started his career in advertising, so delivering creativity has always been his professional purpose. He founded Ellipsis because he saw that technology – virtual and augmented reality, digital effects, holographics, three-dimensional film – could fuse with theatre and music in ways that previously had been relegated to student theatre projects. McGuinness explains that his company 'applies a digital model to a location-based experience. The technology is the servant of the experience, that ultimately it's about creating *human* connections.'[9]

Once an experience is conceived, designed and built, it can be delivered in multiple locations simultaneously. Delivery costs (operating expenses) are much lower than the initial cost of creation (capital expenses) because Ellipsis's variable costs to run an experience include only a small cast of actors (usually requiring about 12 people in all, including front of house) and the venue's rent. A disused warehouse is much cheaper to rent than a West End theatre. Because such theatres are so expensive for hosting a production, a play needs to almost sell out every night in order to make a profit. Not so with the Ellipsis business model, where a Somnai guest would spend £46, half of an average Broadway or West End ticket price. Multiple audiences could pass through each day, and the production can also scale up quickly, exponentially increasing its margins without the same growing additions to fixed costs that a producer would incur with a touring Broadway show.

Confident in the strategy and product, Somnai was a proof of concept, which then emboldened Ellipsis to produce an immersive *War of the Worlds* experience incorporating the 1976 score by composer Jeff Wayne. The audience, again in small groups, huddle under a table in a residence while the Martian machines outside burst through the windows. The guests ride a boat down the Thames to escape the alien scourge with VR headsets transmitting the terrifying scene while wind and water spray across the thrilled group as their boat lurches up and down on a mechanical platform.

When I asked McGuinness about his company's greatest challenge and his concomitant greatest leadership challenge, he reflected, 'Our mission is to figure out how to innovate faster, conquer the incumbent forces, and discover the possible, the uncharted territory. My challenge is simultaneously to be an architect, juggler, visionary and accountant.'[10] His leadership is multi-layered – he plays many roles at the same time. Either the company's spirit reflects McGuinness's approach or vice versa because McGuinness returns repeatedly to the theme of 'layers' in describing an Ellipsis experience, combining elements such as music, wind, water, actors and holograms to etch indelible memories.

In fact, the company researched how lasting memories are made and they learned that the more layers there are to the memory, the stronger it is. McGuinness's job is to climb up and down those layers that are also within the company's strata of digital, scenic, sound and costume designers, coders, directors, researchers and investors. He calls himself an evangelist because 'you need energy, confidence, belief and evidence in equal measure to motivate your employees and inspire your investors'.[11]

The most famous soliloquy in Shakespeare's *As You Like It* is the misanthropic Jaques' monologue, which begins:

All the world's a stage,
And all the men and women merely players...
And one man in his time plays many parts.[12]

It seems appropriate to apply this musing as a metaphor for a creative leader like McGuinness, who in his lifetime, or more accurately every single day, has played many parts. I've been privileged to work across dozens of industries and I've observed clearly that to hold innovation and adaptability in constant balance with commercial realities almost by definition requires the leader to transition with extraordinary dexterity from role to role, from layer to layer, at a frequency that I typically do not see often enough in the executive suite of so-called 'traditional' industries.

Another layer in which McGuinness operates is less about his own role and more about empowering his team, inspiring their innovation and encouraging a dynamic that grows their collective creative capacity. Success along these objectives begins with hiring carefully. McGuinness says, 'I select my directors on their ability to be open to a spectrum of ideas and on their creative confidence to absorb others' ideas and keep their own. I don't want people who think in tunnels. A requisite for our success is a broadening of our perspective. So we need to be confident and eager to teach and learn from one another.'[13] Ellipsis is the epitome of multi-disciplinary collaboration. It is insufficient to hire so-called 'Clevers'[14] and assume that the business's creative capability will be any greater than the sum of its individuals. In fact, if colleagues do not have the inclination to collaborate and be open to playing with one another's ideas, then the organization's innovation capacity may actually be smaller than the sum of its parts, as the dynamic will hinder collective learning and cross-fertilization of concepts and prototypes.

One thing you can do on Monday morning

A common mistake for leaders is to conflate what motivates them with what motivates the individuals in their team. As a result, leaders can struggle to recruit, engage and retain their high performers.[15] For this reason, managers must be intensely curious about why their people chose their respective careers, why they do what they do and why they do it with this organization instead of with any other. Dave Crawford continuously returns to the questions, 'Are you encouraged that you are on the right path? Am I developing you in the right manner and direction for that path?' All manner of actions and development opportunities become clearer and personal based on the answers to those questions.

Too many companies assume that an annual review or personal development plan is based solely on the person's current role, time in role and assumed next role. But careers today are far less linear and predictable than they were even 25 years ago. To be curious about motivation and one's paradigms about work–life, how people like to be managed or how they see their career progressing is to be attuned to motivation. And to be attuned to motivation will facilitate an environment where innovation may thrive.

Do not assume that the answers you may receive to these types of 'purpose' questions are static either. They can and do change over time, and this is increasingly common. So it's necessary to keep returning to asking, sense checking and testing your assumptions if you truly understand your people *today* versus six months ago. I would even suggest beginning every review, development and feedback conversation with these types of questions because they provide very useful context for the manager to adapt and give rationale for *why* they may be giving this feedback or suggesting this development plan beyond the anodyne reason, 'Well, the company says so.'

Any project you give to a direct report will be more engaging to them if you can explain how it fits within their purpose and develops that purpose. There are all manner of projects, shadowing, coaching, mentoring, secondments or international placements that all of a sudden become intriguing if you can create a golden thread between the activity and the individual's purpose. Your approach is of course more human and personal, and you have also helped the person clearly to understand how their company helps them to achieve their dreams and how doing what they do in turn contributes to the organization's mission. There is no greater engagement and retention tool that leaders have at their disposal.

Endnotes

1 Interview with Dave Crawford, 17 July 2020. Dave is now vice president of functional strategy and integration at Virgin Galactic.

2 Joe Rohde, *The Imagineering Story*, directed by Leslie Iwerks (Burbank, CA: Disney, 2019).

3 Interview with Wilsey Mockett, 2022.

4 *Snow White and the Seven Dwarves*, directed by David Hand (Burbank, CA: Disney, 1937).

5 Tom Peters, *A Passion for Excellence: The Leadership Difference* (New York: Random House, 1985).

6 Rohde, *The Imagineering Story*.

7 Richard Farson, *Management of the Absurd: Paradoxes in Leadership* (London: Simon & Schuster, 1997).

8 A couple of other leading-edge companies delivering the highest-quality immersive theatrical experiences in London are Secret Cinema and Gingerline.

9 Interview with Andrew McGuinness in London, 3 March 2020.

10 Ibid.

11 Ibid. McGuinness explained why he listed 'evidence' as one of the qualities he needs to use frequently: 'Leadership means having a clear hypothesis, and you're constantly ferreting out evidence to prove or confound that hypothesis.' In this context, McGuinness is applying the creative principle of experimentation to his business, product and management model.

12 William Shakespeare, *As You Like It*, in *The Riverside Shakespeare*, ed. G Blakemore Evans (Boston: Houghton Mifflin, 1974), II, vii, 139–42.

13 Ibid.

14 Rob Goffee and Gareth Jones, *Clever* (Boston: Harvard Business Review Press, 2009).

15 For more, see my book *Next Generation Leadership* (New York: HarperCollins, 2020).

07
Combining and inspiring ideas
The realm of culinary arts

We must acknowledge that it requires a lot of energy to achieve real innovation. When it comes to invention, we sometimes have to be patient, focused and tolerant of iteration and adaptation. Inspiration can be about finding a brand new idea, but some of the most ground-breaking inventions were novel combinations of existing concepts. So we have inspiration and combination as two avenues to invention. One field in which we can easily observe how ideas travel through these two clear routes is the culinary arts.

In this chapter, we'll look at how world-class chefs ideate to invent Michelin-starred dishes that stretch our usual comprehension of flavours, combinations and cultural influences. We'll also see how corporations utilize the same principles to develop and implement new ideas and even make incremental improvements to legacy products, processes or services.

But before we go further, I should address a question that niggled at me from the earliest days of researching this book. Of all the artistic media that we explore in this book, the culinary craft is perhaps the most troublesome in terms of its artistic credentials. Namely, is cooking ultimately a skill or an art? In the words of the godfather of New York restaurateurs, André Soltner, are chefs really just 'soup merchants'?[1] How much of cooking is tradecraft, the perfection of a set of skills and a deep understanding and practice of the basic building blocks of a cuisine, and how much of it is communicating a story, a life, a dream, a vision, a soul? Eric Ripert, the chef of three Michelin-starred Le Bernardin in New York, has grappled with this question and concluded that there is not only art but even divinity in his craft. 'As a cook and a chef, I'm attempting to convey a message that food is sacred. To realize this in food, I believe, is when cooking becomes art…. Artists are craftsmen with a spiritual message, and cooks may convey spiritual messages as well.'[2] Chef Ferran Adrià of El Bulli, which topped the renowned World's 50 Best Restaurants a record five times, wants his dishes to say something, to stimulate a dialogue. To that extent, his craft is also artistic: 'Cooking not only satisfies a physiological need or provides sensory pleasure, it also elicits important aesthetic responses, anchors them in a story, and establishes an evolution. Ferran… manipulates ingredients like a language which he can model and revitalize so that his creations take a place among other artistic forms.'[3] This humble craftsman concurs that the culinary field can certainly, in its ultimate expressions, offer supreme examples of artistic expression and therefore deserves its place in this book.

What can we learn about creativity from one of the most difficult industries in which to succeed, where 60 per cent of restaurants will fail in the first year and 80 per cent in the first five?[4] At the same time, restaurants are big business. The average American consumer in 2018 spent $660 a month eating out, representing 13 per cent of all household spending.[5] Overall, US restaurant sales climbed to $863 billion in 2019.[6] To put those figures in perspective, US Steel earned $12.9 billion in 2019[7] and Broadway theatre ticket sales that year totalled just $1.43 billion.[8] If a well-executed dish is an art form, then culinary art is the highest-earning medium of all forms. It is therefore a great avenue for exploring the synergy between artistic exploration and commercial reward.

But how common is artistic expression in the culinary field? How much of recipe invention is evolutionary, or just tweaking, and how much is entirely new? I have been fortunate enough to be able to immerse myself in the culinary world: an extended course at Le Cordon Bleu in southern California and later working in business development for a talent management, media and consumer products agency in London that specializes in representing celebrity chefs and lifestyle 'gurus'. In talking regularly with restaurant and television chefs, recipe developers and food journalists at the top of their game, I saw quickly that they each had quite different views about their creative contribution to their field. Some thought they would only add a footnote to the rich culinary heritage that they inherited, maybe a flourish to the vast symphony of cuisine in which they played a lone instrument among thousands. Others saw the possibility to compose a new symphony, cement a legacy, illuminate a new direction. Most radically, some chefs are able to spark new creations by reinventing their whole approach and public perception of what their food is about. In each case, there are lessons for the wider business world on enhancing their creative capacity.

Combinatorial creativity

When asked how they develop their recipes, some chefs subscribe to the 'combinatorial' view. In other words, they combine existing ideas, techniques or ingredients in new or less familiar ways. There are many historical examples of this which culminated in what we today regard as iconic foods. One classic story is that of Antoine Feuchtwanger at the St Louis World's Fair in 1904. Feuchtwanger sold sausages which he called 'frankfurters' after his native Frankfurt. He was losing money because plates and tableware were too expensive, and when he provided gloves to his customers to hold the hot frankfurters he often wouldn't get the gloves back. With the help of his brother, a baker, they created a bread roll that was the right length and height to hold the sausage, and voilà – the hotdog was born![9]

Another iconic dish sprang to life through combinatorial creativity at that same fair. Syrian concessionaire Ernest Hamwi sold waffles. One day, he noticed the ice-cream vendor next door had run out of dishes. A quick conference with this seller, an adjustment to the thickness of the waffle to be able to wrap it around the ice cream, and the world was introduced to the ice-cream cone.[10]

Today, chef Bobby Chinn utilizes such a combinatorial approach with great accomplishment. Chinn's life story is one of combining unlikely experiences. Raised in California, of Chinese and Egyptian heritage and a fluent Arabic speaker, Chinn lived and studied on three continents by the age of ten, worked in finance and even stand-up and improv comedy before moving to Hanoi to open Restaurant Bobby Chinn, an East–West gastronomic celebration, and later the House of Hô in London that showcases traditional Vietnamese flavours with modernized approaches using technology and whimsical presentations. Fans of television cooking programmes have seen Chinn in World Café Asia and as a judge on the Middle East's edition of the cooking competition show 'Top Chef'.

Chinn loved living right in the middle of Vietnam's economic explosion in the mid-1990s before Vietnamese food became hot globally. He called the environment 'the wild, wild East'. Vietnamese food itself is one of the world's great successes of fusion cuisine, showcasing the influences of China, France and the spice trade, which Chinn describes as 'modern cuisine perfected hundreds of years ago'. Chinn teaches his chefs five or six key Vietnamese dishes and simultaneously ensures they can create nuanced sauces by borrowing from both Western and Japanese concepts. The result of this approach produces a wide range of marinades and sauces that can be made consistently and authentically by cooks that have never necessarily even tried Vietnamese food.

The menu at Restaurant Bobby Chinn showcases the diverse mixology of the chef's global life with Californian sensibilities seamlessly pairing Middle Eastern, Indian and Vietnamese flavours with Western techniques. For example, the kitchen uses the tropical guava fruit in a spicy Indian jam that is then used as a glaze for quail in a classic Moroccan bisteeya (a sweet and savoury pie). All the elements are cooked separately and then wrapped in Vietnamese rice paper instead of the traditional filo dough. Another fusion example might be adding wasabi, or Japanese horseradish, to mashed potatoes to add the Asian top note of heat to the base note comfort of a Midwestern American or central European staple, giving you Wasabi Mash!

Wasabi Mash

400g peeled, chopped potatoes

1/3 cup cream (could substitute whole milk, but why would you!)

3 tbsp unsalted butter

3 tsp wasabi paste

Salt and pepper to taste

Boil the potatoes in salted water until tender. Drain and leave to steam dry. Add to a saucepan over low heat and begin mashing gently with a large fork or a potato masher (or ideally put the potatoes through a ricer before putting over heat). Slowly incorporate the cream and butter as you mash. Take your time and be gentle. As soon as the mash is the texture you desire, incorporate the wasabi, season and serve.

Chinn was toying with putting a Southeast Asian twist on the classic Peruvian dish of ceviche – fish cooked with an acid such as lime juice rather than with heat. He wanted a perfect balance of sweet and sour and realized why traditional recipes weren't giving him the desired result – the native limes in Peru have a different ratio of sweet to sour. So to get that balance right and to introduce Vietnam into the flavour equation, Chinn looked to the mangosteen, native to Vietnam and known as the 'queen of fruits', which is similar to lychee but sweeter and more delicate. That sweetness coupled with the limes that Chinn could procure locally would hit the right ratio of sweet to sour that Peruvian limes could achieve on their own, but the mangosteen would also introduce that Southeast Asian nuance to the dish. Finally, Chinn added chilli and avocado for balance and shiso, a herb common in Japan that tastes like a combination of mint and basil, instead of coriander. And there you have tropical Asian ceviche! But before all the combinatorial creativity, the key is to master those basic flavours, recipes and mother sauces. As Chinn says, 'A cook is a mechanic who finds peace in repetition. *Then* you have the right to dream.'[11] This philosophy is a helpful one for the business leader: make sure that your people understand the elemental components of your products and services, such as their histories, brand values and DNA, value proposition, non-negotiable product features, intended buyers, why those consumers choose to buy over offerings from competitors, and how they prefer to buy. Then your team can play with different combinations and ratios to create and adapt products and services.

Combining previously separate concepts may also occur because of emerging market desires or even market restrictions. For example, Chinn saw a wealth of amazing Asian recipes that used pork and at the same time millions of Muslims living in Southeast Asia who could not enjoy them. He thought of the Scotch eggs (hard-boiled eggs wrapped in sausage meat, then rolled in breadcrumbs and deep fried) that he had enjoyed as a student in the United Kingdom and reimagined the Scotch egg in a vegetarian version with Vietnamese flavours. He substituted the sausage meat with cut cellophane (rice) noodles, five-spice powder and mushrooms to provide the umami[12] that the meat would otherwise add. He bound this mixture with beaten egg, rolled it in breadcrumbs and deep fried it as normal. Then Chinn asked himself, 'Why can't I make shumai (dumplings) with chicken instead of with pork?' He set his chefs on the task of creating tasty chicken shumai without losing the moisture and succulence that the pork would have provided.

Beyond combining disparate ideas to innovate, Chinn's process also illustrates the importance of knowing the customer and using their lead to inspire the next new product or service. LEGO doggedly applies this lesson. Former Brand Manager Per Enggrob Larsen remembers, 'We tried very much to spend a lot of time outside the office, meeting with people stocking shelves, talking to consumers in the aisle and just asking them, "Why did you pick that item? Why did you go over there?" We almost formalized the number of days that everyone in each marketing team had to spend with a sales representative, driving around to shops. We didn't really have that many resources to do focus groups, but we made sure all teams spent a lot of time driving around with the salespeople. Most marketing people don't like doing that. They like being in the office or with the agencies in big cities or conducting market research with a specialist agency. It's always been a struggle to get people to leave the office to drive around with sales representatives and approach consumers in the aisle, but it's so important.' The power of 'Display', as Pixar called the process of inviting collaborative feedback, is actually another form of combinatorial creativity itself. In this case, it's exploring multiple perspectives or disciplines in order to refine an offer.

Returning to the culinary field, chef Alain Passard of Paris's three Michelin-starred L'Arpège describes combinatorial creativity in how he invented his dessert Bouquet of Roses. This dish started with the idea of a classic apple tarte tatin but introduces a new, simple but purposeful technique in how the apples are sliced. Passard cuts each apple into a single, wide ribbon, rolls it into a rose shape and nestles that rose into a pastry case. He explains his reason: 'I don't want to do the same thing every day. I never saw myself making an apple pie in the same, traditional way forever... I needed to find something else. I had the idea of a ribbon shaped like a rose that you put inside the pie. In fact, it's a design. There is something new to it.'[13] That novelty alone can be gratifying to both cook and diner. But there is also a technical reason why Passard's invention works, according to one of his chefs at L'Arpège: 'We [can] have a pie like one we might have at our grandmother's, but [here]... we have an apple pie from the mind of Alain Passard. He unrolls the entire apple like a ribbon and turns it into fabric. He rolls it into a rose. This works on the apple's texture. This preserves some crunch.'[14] Diners recognize tarte tatin and have a sense memory of that dish, yet visually and texturally experience something unexpected that challenges their conception of tarte tatin and creates an inner dialogue about how the apple can be enjoyed in a tatin preparation.

We can return to LEGO for an example of this process of combinatorial creativity in action. In 2006, LEGO launched MINDSTORMS, which was essentially a component, a programmable brick containing a microprocessor and screen which, when combined with other sophisticated LEGO parts like motors and sensors, allowed the consumer to turn their LEGO constructions into robots.[15] The launch of MINDSTORMS NXT was a crowdsourced effort, asking LEGO's research and development engineers and a group of LEGO super-user customers to invent and test different products, combining the MINDSTORMS components in unanticipated and exciting ways.

The combinatorial, crowdsourced brainstorming that we observe with LEGO MINDSTORMS is also a technique that

Bobby Chinn uses when improving his dishes and techniques. For example, Chinn wanted to create a very slow-cooked egg but with a hard white. Most recipes for the 'very slow-cooked egg' call for immersing the egg in a temperature-controlled water bath at 64.5 degrees Celsius for an hour. The problem is that while the yolk is runny and the egg is cooked, the egg white can still have an unpleasant gelatinous consistency. So Chinn tackled the problem once and for all when he found a willing group at a food and wine festival in Hawaii a few years ago.

Students from a local culinary school were tasked with assisting the guest chefs at the festival, but the chefs weren't really taking up the offer. Chinn observed the students just sitting around. Here was an untapped, problem-solving crack team! He approached the students, explained what he wanted from his slow-cooked egg and encouraged them to try as many variations of the recipe that they wished in order to get the outcome he sought. Chinn explains, 'I like to ask people to solve problems. These kids had nothing else to do, so I asked them to cook 20 eggs differently.' The students not only applied many diverse techniques but also collaborated by sharing their observations of each attempt with one another. And sure enough, the students cracked the problem, no pun intended. After cooking the egg in a water bath in the usual manner for an hour, one enterprising student then stopped the cooking process by shocking the egg in ice water and then immersing it in fully boiling water for just one minute. That hardened the egg white without compromising the beautiful silken, molten texture of the yolk. Chinn observed, 'The students were so proud, they didn't want to leave my stand!'

Wholly new creativity

Some chefs approach invention by aiming for the completely new, the hitherto unknown dish, technique or ingredient. Two themes that become quickly apparent in exploring how these innovations were brought to life are that first, the invention process tends to take longer, and second, the chefs in question have a dedicated research and development kitchen. In hindsight, both of these conditions make intuitive sense. Truly novel innovation takes time and dedicated resources.

On the theme of letting evolution take its time, consider the story of how the pioneering Ferran Adrià of Spain's El Bulli, in its day repeatedly heralded as the world's best restaurant and receiving 2 million reservation requests for 8,000 places every year, introduced foam as a new component to the culinary landscape. He remembers, 'The idea came to us in a juice bar one day when we noticed the froth on the tops of the glasses of juice. Beginning in 1990, we had been working on the idea of creating a lighter mousse with a more intense flavour than possible in traditional mousses, and in the three years that followed we did a lot of experimenting. To enable us to make foams, it was crucial that we had a siphon; this was the utensil that would make our dream come true. Our first experiment involved placing a consommé in the siphon. The product retained its consistency, which we attributed to its natural gelatine. It then seemed a logical step to add sheets of gelatine to products that neither contained nor produced their own gelatine. In 1994 we added gelatine to a purée of white beans and put the mix through the siphon. This was the first foam that we took out to diners in our restaurant, and we served it with sea urchin. All of these were savoury foams, but the obvious next step was to branch out into sweet confections. Now chefs have the option of using cold foams to make wonderful tarts instantly. The pastry stays crisp because it is filled with foam at the very last moment, so that it has no time to become damp, and the texture of the foam itself makes the tarts very light.'[16]

Note that in Adrià's timeline, the development of foam as an ingredient, before it was ready to put on a plate in front of a paying customer, took four years, and the chef had the advantage of a dedicated research and development (R&D) team. In fact, El Bulli was open only six months a year, while the other six months were wholly focused on creating new dishes. Originally, the six months of operation per year were to accommodate the bulk of patrons who arrived during the summer holidays. Later, the team needed six months to develop the next year's completely new menu. I'm not suggesting that a business must shut down in order to invent new offers to market, but I am proposing that a company might consider having one team exploiting and improving current products or services while another simultaneously invents the next generation of propositions that create value for customers.

The El Bulli definition of creativity was borrowed from celebrated French chef Jacques Maximin: 'Creativity is not copying.'[17] To accomplish the completely new, at pace and at volume, requires time. In almost every example I've encountered of wholly novel invention, the creator put aside significant time and other resources (people, budget, etc) to the task. Chef Heston Blumenthal of the three Michelin-starred and delightfully original Fat Duck in the United Kingdom also enjoys a separate, dedicated kitchen and team for R&D. Unlike combinatorial creativity or incremental evolution, the brand-new demands space for the divine spark of genesis.

The El Bulli research team also meticulously documented their experiments so that the overall learning, the wisdom of the kitchen, grew alongside the burgeoning repertoire of innovative dishes, including Carrot Foam with Hazelnut Foam-Air and Córdoba Spices, or Monkfish Liver Fondue with Ponzu and White Sesame Flavoured Kumquat. The R&D group also codified the principles through which to explore new plates or flavours. These included 'association, inspiration, adaptation, deconstruction and minimalism' so that the creative process immediately had a direction and focus.[18] Finally, the team converged and documented their overall process for developing any dish:

1 Someone in the creative team has an idea for a new technique, concept or dish.

2 The idea is developed using one or more of the principles listed above.

3 Tests are carried out and recorded in the creative notebooks.

4 The tests are analysed using both personal palate and flavour combination tables.

5 A full dish is prototyped in the restaurant's kitchen.

6 The new dish is served to customers; their reactions or observations are noted.

7 Based on these observations, the dish is adapted if need be.

8 Once finalized, the dish is recorded in the general catalogue.[19]

Adrià recognized early on that creativity without order can be chaos, and he converged on the method and lenses by which innovation would happen at El Bulli. This structure facilitated the training of new chefs, sped up the volume of creative outputs and ensured that the novel had some theme or direction that the executive chef had already endorsed.

Just a little bit of direction has an enormously positive impact on creativity. Of course, it's a fine balance between giving freedom and providing direction, but it's worthwhile to work at finding the right balance for you and your team. One lesson that the leader can always remind their team is that innovation is 'creativity plus added value'. In other words, before we get excited about a new idea, what is the additional value that idea may contribute to the customer or business?

By providing the lenses through which one can create, Adrià did not have to rely solely on his own creative capacity. He engineered the environment whereby the whole brigade was employed to the task of invention, not just execution. The team was as responsible for El Bulli's legend as Adrià himself. Decades before El Bulli, famed chef André Soltner also acknowledged how critical the whole team was to the success of his Lutèce, the New York bastion of culinary excellence for decades: 'I need good chefs. I need good ingredients. I need good waiters. I need good dishwashers. On one night I will serve one hundred dinners. If the plates are not ready on time, if they are not warmed, if they are not placed precisely right, then it will not work. Our secret is that it works well most nights. Lutèce is not a restaurant of the chef but of the whole crew.'[20] Many customers may consider that the success and consistency in a great restaurant are down to the executive chef, whereas it's at least equally due to the brigade's excellence. Chinn, Adrià and Soltner all recognize that.

This concept is even more important in traditional, hierarchical business environments because the more senior the leader, the more their attention is drawn inwards, managing internal stakeholders, departments and shareholders. The leader's team usually enjoys a more accurate perspective of customers' needs and so are better placed to innovate in the most relevant fashion. It is a disadvantageous symptom of hierarchy – the more effective that employees are with customers, the more likely it is that they will be promoted and therefore distanced from those customers, yet they are still the ones who judge how those customers should be served. With every passing year, however, the leader's judgement is based on an ever-diminishing relevance of personal experience with customers.

Reinvention for inspiration

Alain Passard, at L'Arpège in Paris, used to be known as the king of meat preparations. But he could not maintain the creative state that he desired by being limited to animal protein. He felt lost, stifled, stuck. He instinctively recognized that he needed time to reflect, to refresh and reinvent himself, or he would never have a hope of continuing to invent cuisine at the highest level. This is not a unique condition for harried chefs alone; it's very common among executives. We often feel that we're hamsters on a wheel and we can't get off, even though we know we have to change. That's often the most effective yet hardest step to take. Passard took it, and in so doing he revealed to himself a humble little world that until then he had practically ignored. And he discovered inspiration – wholly new ideas.

In his garden while on sabbatical in 1998, Passard discovered vegetables. Of course, he had always cooked with vegetables, but to make them the stars on the plate would be to create a new world in which to play and a new identity to communicate to the world. Passard recollects, 'When your senses are deprived of nourishment, that's when you should begin to worry. I was in a period of rupture. I needed rest. What happened to my life as a cook? I needed time to think. What I knew was that animal flesh was done. I realized I wanted to do something else, to change my job. I didn't know what had happened to my life. It was a very painful time. [My sabbatical] was an important year because I had gotten some rest, some distance. This retrospection allowed me to have this [new] idea. A beet can be cooked in a crust of salt like meat. A stalk of celery can be smoked. An onion can be flambeed. A carrot can be grilled.... I was enthusiastic again. I wanted to create again. That made me very happy – a new outlook. I had new tastes, new smells, new sounds, the sounds of different cooking. And for me, that was the most important thing. I found pleasure in cooking again.'

Passard wanted a vegetarian menu, removing all the dishes that earned the three Michelin stars. It was a little shocking and many of his employees and customers thought that L'Arpège was finished, that Passard would lose everything: the restaurant, the customers, the stars. But he was determined and even went to tell the Michelin Guide staff what he was doing. He recounts, 'I told [the Michelin director] that I wanted to work with vegetables. I told him, "Listen, sir, I've made my choice. Now you make yours." I said goodbye and left. I was badly perceived. The restaurant started losing clients. The critics were not kind. I had to learn again. I was working day and night to prove that we could do a vegetable cuisine. It was the year 2000. Everyone was waiting for the new Michelin Guide: "Arpège will lose its stars! They are just doing carrots and turnips!" And… we kept our stars, and we still have them. I live in a country that loves a little piece of fish, a little piece of duck. But I found the right balance in the end.'[21]

In a Parisian three-star restaurant 20 years ago, to say that you would stop serving meat was practically an insult to French culture, a crime against the state! Passard's conversion to vegetable cuisine was *insane bravery*, a real game of Russian roulette, because he could have crashed.[22] But in reinventing himself and the way he perceived himself as a chef, Passard changed the way people eat. He legitimized vegetables as worthy stars rather than support players several years before such a concept was widely adopted. In taking that risk, Passard demonstrates that the creative genius sometimes tells the marketplace what it has been missing, *even when customers don't recognize it themselves*. That's risky. It takes guts and confidence in your vision, but it can move an entire market, an entire industry, in a different direction. And of course, we celebrate the pioneer who led the way.

If we turn to a corporate example, Netflix reinvented itself, created a wholly new offer to the consumer, and so ensured its sector leadership rather than obsolescence. Always the disruptor, Netflix almost singlehandedly put Blockbuster out of business by pioneering a DVD delivery business model. Netflix could have sat back and enjoyed healthy margins and growing profitability for several more years by simply exploiting that strategy. But the company saw that the future of home entertainment lay in streaming video and so it invested its resources into a virtual entertainment model. In reinventing itself, Netflix reinvented the entire industry. To this day, Netflix enjoys first-mover advantages in its market dominance, but those advantages are never permanent. With increasing competitors and decreasing subscribers, even Netflix cannot rest on its laurels. Novel approaches are slowly adopted by others over time and so the creative capacity of the company must always be called upon for continuous invention and reinvention.

Netflix was not the first forecaster of the evolution to streaming video, but it was early off the mark to exploit that trend. Even back in the 1980s, researchers at telephone and communications giant AT&T projected the bandwidth that would be available in American homes over the next several decades and the amount of bandwidth that would be needed to deliver full motion video over a data network rather than over the air via broadcast. Critically, those researchers forecast that the two trends would intersect in about 2005. That was when it would become technically feasible to stream high-quality videos into our homes, and so it turned out to be. YouTube was founded in February 2005 and bought less than two years later by Google for $1.65 billion.[23] Today, 300 hours of video content are uploaded to YouTube every minute. Netflix, which at the time of writing had 223 million users,[24] started streaming its content in 2007. While we couldn't have predicted 40 years ago the vast array of opportunities that video streaming would enable, by 2000 it was apparent it would be a gamechanger and represented an existential threat to the traditional television industry. Netflix was among the first to adapt to the inevitable. The company didn't get everything right on the introduction of streaming, but it didn't have to be perfect for its customers to appreciate the obvious convenience and service advantages while Netflix ironed out the wrinkles. Perfection is not a precondition for invention or reinvention.

On perfection

Chef André Soltner also spoke to an important concept in pursuing excellence when he said 'it works well most nights', the idea that perfection is worthy of the pursuit itself but may not ever be fully attainable. As Martha Ortiz, the chef at Mexico City's Dulce Patria, describes, 'Creativity becomes a vessel for us to deliver the flavours of our food. I don't believe the perfect dish exists, but as chefs, part of our craft is striving for perfection hoping to create a masterpiece.'[25] Or as chef Ana Roš of Slovenia's Hiša Franko observes, 'You dream about perfection and are always on the hunt, but… imperfection is the engine for evolution. I do not believe there are signature dishes that should never be changed or modified. Evolution, like the rest of nature, is unstoppable and we must always adapt to change.'[26]

There are a few reasons that we never achieve perfection. First, perfection is in the eye of the beholder; nothing would be perceived as perfect to everyone. Second, short of robotic manufacturing, no output will always be identical to its predecessors. It is as important to acknowledge this in cooking as it is in music, theatre, painting or professional services such as management consulting. The nature of human-produced repetition inevitably includes variation, which by definition precludes perfection. Third, one never experiences the same sensation twice: 'All sensations are modified through repetition, for the very fact of recurrence alters the nature of the sensation.'[27]

Just as one chef would not invent a dish in exactly the same way as another colleague, the culinary arts teach us at least three approaches to innovation. Perhaps the fastest method is to combine one idea with a previously unrelated one and brainstorm what that marriage could resemble, such as Bobby Chinn's Wasabi Mash. This routine produces a high volume of new concepts, which is always desirable. A second process is the singular, novel idea, and the stories of these chefs demonstrate that this takes time and cannot be forced. A new ingredient such as Ferran Adrià's foam required proactively creating the space for the concept to gestate and the patience to iterate. The third method is personal reinvention, such as Alain Passard's philosophical pivot to vegetarian cuisine. Our choices, routines, habits and assumptions can stifle creativity if we do not occasionally step back and reflect on which of these help us and which are no longer useful. Redefining what we do or how we wish the world to perceive us can open new avenues and in itself realize personal adaptability.

One thing you can do on Monday morning

I encounter so many senior executives who know that the enterprise is ready for a change but can't devote their attention to it. A suggestion, which is really not so very radical: every leader needs to take a one to four week sabbatical every year – but a thoughtful one, to look back, look ahead and look inward, stopping all other activity. Not a holiday but time turned to reflection and reinvention. Novelist Gertrude Stein said, 'It takes a lot of time to be a genius. You have to sit around so much doing nothing, really doing nothing.'[28]

Chefs move from restaurant to restaurant a lot. Is this the restlessness of the creative spirit, the need to reinvent? Yes, at least partially. A new environment allows individuals to consider themselves in a new light. Many chefs speak about their concern with getting lost in someone else's vision, or even their own, outdated vision for a particular restaurant that no longer represents who they are. A fresh, clean break is sometimes in order. Now, I'm not suggesting that you must change employers in order to reinvent, though it is worth considering every now and then. At the least, a sabbatical will afford you the time and space to consider whether you need to find a new environment for yourself, to create a different dynamic or leadership impact within your current environment, or if you need to apply new lenses or principles to your creative challenges in order to consider solutions through fresh perspectives.

And another thing...

There was so much rich inspiration in my interviews for this chapter that I must include another practical suggestion. We discussed combinatorial creativity, which occurs more often than birthing a singularly new idea into the world. Three Michelin star chef Thomas Keller of the French Laundry in California and Per Se in New York distinguishes between 'influence' which comes from countless sources around us and 'inspiration' which comes from within and is much rarer.[29]

In order to keep evaluating combinations of ideas that you hadn't brought together before, make matchmaking a habit. One exercise that you can do on your own or with your team is to draw two lines on a large sheet of paper, creating three equally sized columns. At the top of the left-hand column write 'From Our World'. At the top of the second column write 'From Other Worlds'. And at the top of the third column write 'Innovations'. In the first column, list the themes, products, services, features, business models or processes that you want to refresh or reinvent. It's best to have a focus and cover just one genre such as 'features'. In the second column, write completely unrelated things, people, ideas or influences. The more seemingly random, the better. In the last column, brainstorm what would happen if you combined each item in column one with an influence from column two.

For example, a team at an office furniture company may want to create a new design for their desk lamp. Their exercise may look something like the below.

From our world – our lamp	From other worlds	Innovations
Straight tube from the base to the shade	Salvador Dalí	The tube coils into a knot in the middle before continuing up to the shade
Lamp shade is monochrome	Jackson Pollock	Spatter several bright colours onto the shade; every lamp is different

From our world – our lamp	From other worlds	Innovations
A switch on the base turns the light on and off	iPhone	No switch = cleaner design. You turn the light on and off using an app on your phone
A cord plugs the lamp into an outlet	Tesla	No cord. The lamp is battery operated, so it's more mobile

And so on…. Of course, you can apply every influence from the second column to each item in the first column to surface more possible innovations for each feature. For instance, how would Dalí, Pollock, the iPod and Tesla each alter or improve the cord element on the lamp? Many innovations won't be attractive or feasible. It's not about perfection but about volume to increase the odds of discovering a good idea. If you get one interesting idea to develop further from each iteration of this exercise, then you've made a great new habit out of innovation and adaptability. You've improved your own creativity and that of your team.

Endnotes

1 Greg Morabito, 'Mimi Sheraton recalls André Soltner working the floor', *Eater New York*, 30 August 2012.

2 Eric Ripert and Michael Ruhlman, *A Return to Cooking* (New York: Artisan, 2002), 319.

3 Ferran Adrià, Albert Adrià and Juli Soler, *A Day at El Bulli* (London: Phaidon Press, 2008), 400.

4 Jarrett Bellini, 'The No. 1 thing to consider before opening a restaurant', CNBC.com, 15 March 2016, https://www.cnbc.com/2016/01/20/heres-the-real-reason-why-most-restaurants-fail.html# (archived at https://perma.cc/9G7C-VTGT)

5 Christy Bieber, 'Average food spending tops 10% of income', USA Today, 1 May 2020, https://eu.usatoday.com/story/money/2020/05/01/average-food-spending-save-money/111623736/ (archived at https://perma.cc/KJ6B-8SCS)

6 Lauren Stine, 'Restaurant spending to hit record $863B in 2019', RestaurantDive.com, 20 August 2019, https://www.restaurantdive.com/news/restaurant-spending-to-hit-record-863b-in-2019/561243/ (archived at https://perma.cc/X8BA-V6TQ)

7 Statista.com, 'Global steel industry – U.S Steel Corporation's revenue 2012–2019', 8 May 2020, https://www.statista.com/statistics/198599/global-net-sales-of-united-states-steel-corporation-since-2006/ (archived at https://perma.cc/SRX4-QMPQ)

8 Statista.com, 'Gross revenue of Broadway shows in New York from 2006 to 2019', 2 July 2020, https://www.statista.com/statistics/193006/broadway-shows-gross-revenue-since-2006/ (archived at https://perma.cc/N664-3GH3)

9 Wikiwand, https://www.wikiwand.com/en/Hot_dog_bun (archived at https://perma.cc/UTY8-2QRS)

10 International Dairy Foods Association, https://www.idfa.org/the-history-of-the-ice-cream-cone (archived at https://perma.cc/4L47-5Z4U)

11 Interview with Bobby Chinn, 22 January 2020.

12 Umami has been recognized as the fifth basic flavour element that the human tongue can detect. It is often described as 'meatiness', though it is also found in parmesan, tomatoes and seaweed. The original four flavour elements are sweet, sour, salt and bitter.

13 Alain Passard, 'Chef's Table France', Season 1, Episode 1, directed by David Gelb, Netflix, 2016.

14 Ibid.

15 http://www.legoengineering.com/platform/nxt/ (archived at https://perma.cc/J8WA-LL4F)

16 Ferran Adrià, 'Foams', in *The Cook's Book*, ed. Jill Norman (London: DK, 2005), 60.

17 Adrià, F, Adrià, A and Soler J, *A Day at El Bulli* (London: Phaidon Press, 2008).

18 Ibid, 136.

19 Ibid, 64.

20 Fred Ferretti, 'The art of creating great restaurants', *The New York Times*, 25 November 1979.

21 Passard, 'Chef's Table France'.

22 Ibid.

23 Associated Press, 'Google buys YouTube for $1.65 billion', NBC News, 9 October 2006, https://www.nbcnews.com/id/wbna15196982 (archived at https://perma.cc/P5M8-JS6C)

24 Statista.com, 'Number of Netflix paid subscribers worldwide from 1st quarter 2013 to 3rd quarter 2022', https://www.statista.com/statistics/250934/quarterly-number-of-netflix-streaming-subscribers-worldwide/ (archived at https://perma.cc/M8RP-ZHKA)

25 Rahim Kanani, *A Wealth of Insight: The World's Best Chefs on Creativity, Leadership, and Perfection* (Black Truffle Press, 2019), 130.

26 Ibid, 23.

27 Suzanne Guerlac, *Thinking in Time: An Introduction to Henri Bergson* (Ithaca, NY: Cornell University Press, 2006), 73.

28 Theartstory.org, https://www.theartstory.org/influencer/stein-gertrude/life-and-legacy/ (archived at https://perma.cc/TK6V-CRPS)

29 Thomas Keller, *The French Laundry, Per Se* (New York: Artisan, 2020), 55.

08
Picture perfect
The realm of art and imagery

Businesses are historically poor when it comes to using creativity to inspire and transform their people internally. How, then, can we expect that they will succeed in competing creatively externally? One way in which leaders typically fail to inspire their people is an over-indulgence of figures, tables, deadlines and death by email. Simple imagery can be stickier, infinitely more memorable, and can communicate emotional messages with a power that a memo could never duplicate. The brain processes and retains visual information much more easily than verbal input and in fact can process visual information 60,000 times faster than text.[1] We had hundreds of thousands more years of practice responding to images before our brains adapted to reading.

Visual art is a severely underutilized medium for advancing messages and promoting new ideas. It also is a valuable tool for coalescing team, departmental or organizational missions, for long-term strategy and for encouraging change. Organized religion has understood for thousands of years that creating iconic imagery assists in telling stories, teaching parables and history, and embedding lessons.

I interviewed artists for their first-hand reflections and observed how they deliver art workshops to corporate audiences to discover comfort with ambiguity and search for clarity regarding change or the future. One artist who facilitates such workshops, Peter Moolan-Feroze, has helped executives and teams envision their horizons and consider their relationships to change through painting. He explains how these workshops have accelerated transformation and agility by focusing and reshaping participants' conceptions of their organizations and even of themselves. Then we will turn to corporate examples such as drinks company Suntory, which has used imagery to communicate and reinforce direction externally and to catalyze new and different conversations internally.

While we rely on writing for much of our communication today, much ancient writing began with pictorial representation, such as ancient Egyptian hieroglyphics. In fact, there is still one remaining pictographic system of writing in the world – Dongba, used by the indigenous Naxi people in southwest China.

Imagery is embedded into human history, heritage and instinct and is thus an incredibly useful tool for influencing and making messages stick. Beyond the tactical reasoning to incorporate art and imagery deeper into corporate life, artist Giles Ford argues that art helps people connect with, rather than separate from, their humanity in their work.[2] Ford's career encompasses how art can unlock creativity and self-awareness in business. As a painter whose work is shown in galleries around the world, and as an educator and executive facilitator, Ford sees every day how companies suffer from a culture of fear, control and compliance, which causes a lack of imagination and dreaming. Leaders live as a sliver of who they are or could be. The additional tragedy is that this state is unnatural; creativity is a natural state of being and wellbeing. In the corporate world of today, Ford observes that the creative individual usually occupies the place of the 'peculiar misfit'. To maintain that position, you have to ask yourself if you can be brave enough to embrace that peculiarity that others would reject.

If they cannot accept the creative misfit as a change agent, businesses might instead introduce new ideas under the guise of 'training'. Ford observes that he is frequently brought in to deliver such training because his clients' previous curricula were 10–15 years behind what their people needed in order to be more relevant today. That previous training was also typically delivered more as a science than as an art, thus was one-dimensional and therefore less impactful. To envision new possibilities, futures, products, services and ways of working is to tap into inspiration. It's visceral. Ford notes that generally such ideation in business is too cognitive and superficial because executives usually hate ambiguity. However, most artists *love* ambiguity. Therefore, art can be a useful tool to imagine what might be possible precisely because it embraces starting the necessary work before you know exactly where you're going. To unearth the true present and potential future state of your company or your team, and your own assumptions implicit in those diagnoses, you have to reach into your subconscious. Manifesting what is invisible is intuitive and art is *all about* intuition. Drawing what you cannot express therefore unlocks those invisible barriers.

Drawing into the future

Roger Minton has held a huge variety of human resources (HR) roles, often as head of talent or leadership development, with organizations as diverse as Anglo American, SABIC, Petrofac and BUPA. There is little related to talent management and engagement that Minton has not seen. He recalls that one of the most impactful team meetings he was ever part of used art to accelerate transformation.[3] He was working with an organization that had been through a tumultuous time, having to make redundancies of about 50 per cent of the HR function. This took about two and a half weeks from start to finish, creating new job roles, allowing everyone to apply for their preferred role and then learning who was staying and who was going. The first thing the head of the department did after that turmoil was to assemble the remaining HR leadership team of 12 colleagues and ask them to draw their experience and how they were feeling. Minton recollects that this was one of the most cathartic things he's ever done. As you can imagine, there were quite a lot of black clouds in his drawing but also bits of sun here and there. Everybody did the exercise differently. There were no constraints other than everyone used a pen and paper. That kind of artistic expression was very powerful in illustrating how people were feeling, what they'd been though, and then leading of course to the valuable discussion of how they were to get back to a sunnier future.

When the team session began, the expectation was that it was going to be a regular meeting. No one knew that they were in for anything more than a briefing and a PowerPoint presentation on the future. So the initial reaction was one of surprise to be presented with this idea of 'We really want to know how you're feeling about this. This has been a painful journey for all of us. We want to give you a different way to articulate how it has been for you'. Minton was deeply impressed with that message and the diverse ways in which people represented their thoughts and feelings in their drawings. Some people wrote words if they weren't comfortable drawing, but most did express their feelings graphically. That exercise led into a conversation of 'Look at these drawings and reflect on what we've been through. Let's acknowledge it'. That approach is so powerful because there's often survivor's guilt in those situations: 'It could have been me. Why wasn't it?' Minton notes, 'Once you acknowledge that, you then feel more ready to plot out the future, how it's going to look, and you can leave some of the residual negative emotion behind.' Using art helped the team to bring out what was happening under the surface, allowing this change conversation to integrate emotion and reason.

Art for renewal and transformation

Perhaps we think of creativity as a product of a lifetime of cultivation and therefore is too unwieldy to introduce into the boardroom. However, recall the example from Chapter 1 where research demonstrated that creativity is something with which you're born and then develop or repress throughout your lifetime. But you can always rediscover it. It's odd that some people say 'I'm not creative' when put outside their comfort zone. We need to demystify creativity since it's a natural state. Artist and executive facilitator Peter Moolan-Feroze says, 'There's a joy in not having to be an expert and in rediscovering that. For business people, this is often about renewal and reframing how one sees oneself in order to return to creativity.'[4] Helping the busy executive to do this through the medium of art is to help them move their perspectives and preferences further to the right along several spectra:

Words	$\rightarrow$	Images
Introspection	$\rightarrow$	Empathy
Adult	$\rightarrow$	Child
Observation	$\rightarrow$	Intuition
Replicate	$\rightarrow$	Explore

What holds us back from moving to the right? Moolan-Feroze points out that we tend to overweigh experience: 'Expertise locks us in, our ego rises and makes us fearful of stepping outside of that state. Expertise is important, but genuine creativity might include putting oneself in the shoes of the beginner. That can be scary and is a primary reason we don't innovate, so we can unlock that fear by using art to explore different parts of the self which are not so judgemental, where there is comfort in being wrong.' Or perhaps we could say comfort in pivoting from 'impossible' to 'not impossible'. That requires the right environment where creativity can reflow. As Evan Williams, co-founder, former chairman and CEO of Twitter, said, 'I definitely think people can learn how to be creative, but I think for the most part people unlearn how to do it.'[5] To create the right environment to help with this very challenge, Moolan-Feroze works with companies and executive education groups at business schools to facilitate playful exercises that tease out the participants' perceptions of their realities and sometimes of themselves.

For example, executives spend a lot of time trying to get better at leading change since their companies are in a constant state of flux. So Moolan-Feroze leads an exercise that helps senior managers reveal how and what they think about change itself. In this exercise, he asks them to draw a white coffee cup that he places at the front of the room. Next to the drawing, he encourages the group to write or draw their feelings and observations about the cup, then write a poem to a child about the cup. Then Moolan-Feroze asks his group to draw the cup again through the lens of the poem they've just composed. Now the participants are drawing not just the cup but their feelings and perceptions as they evolved throughout their poems. They have to reach for a higher understanding of their own philosophy about transformation. On one programme, an executive threw down his pastels, exclaiming, 'This is ridiculous, a waste of time!' He was struggling to express himself outside of relying on traditional expertise. While this man didn't see the point of the exercise on that day, a year later Moolan-Feroze received an email from the executive saying he'd taken a cup home and put it on his mantlepiece to remind him to be more openminded.

Symbols in Suntory

The more we look, the more examples we can find of visual art and imagery helping to move an organization's perceptions forward. Consider the case study of Suntory, the global beverage company. I was directing Suntory's Beyond Borders programme, a corporate executive development initiative in collaboration with London Business School. One of those participants, Carol Robert, who is now the chief operating officer of Suntory Beverage and Food for Great Britain and Ireland, recalls, 'We had such a rich experience through diverse learning and connections. We were discussing breakthrough leadership and innovative mindsets with Professor Gary Hamel in one session, and afterward we brainstormed and came up with the idea of creating an iconic and symbolic visual reference to the programme that we as the "founding" group could use as a legacy for and reminder of the course. Suntory had historically given a lapel pin to only the most senior members of the company once they reached a certain level and normally only if they also attended the annual conference with the top leadership. We thought that we could create an equally symbolic pin that was a clear demonstration of being an emerging future global leader.'[6]

One proposal for the pin was in the shape of a katana, the samurai's sword of feudal Japan, symbolizing the group's commitment to 'cut' bureaucracy.[7] The session with Hamel discussed how bureaucracy in all its forms – a multi-layered organizational design, too many permissions required to try something new, difficulty getting a little bit of resource to run an experiment – can shrink a company's capacity for innovation and adaptability. If those two competencies were the hallmarks of Suntory's original success and the precursors to its future competitiveness, then the leadership community had to banish bureaucracy. Of course, this katana symbol did not communicate the entire plan, but it would serve as a daily reminder among the company's senior leaders of their substantial objective to refresh the corporate culture.

Another proposal acknowledged that there were so many other valuable lessons on the programme, and the alumni who came from so many different functions and countries would each prioritize a theme that was most relevant for their context. The pin in this case would need to remind the individual about the programme, but would allow each person to personalize what they took from the memory. The design of this pin used an image of the globe with the Beyond Borders programme logo extending out from it to emphasize the distinct, international nature of the group. This design was ultimately selected.

Robert remembers being given this pin at the following Suntory global leaders' conference: 'A small group of attendees wore this pin instead of the Suntory pin, which created quite some attention and got people talking. At this conference, we were seen to be somehow unique and elite given only a small number had this different pin.' The pin enhanced the participants' profile within the company, and it importantly helped them to remember the behaviours and habits to which they committed despite the hurly burly of the day-to-day back in the office.

Art as metaphor

Another corporate example that uses art as a metaphor to embrace new ways to think about how one contributes value comes from Quest International, which produced flavours and scents for consumer brands before its acquisition by Givaudan in 2006. The oral care division within Quest asked Peter Moolan-Feroze to help them explore the concept of their essence and that of their products through graphic art. After workshopping with Moolan-Feroze, the team ultimately used the style of painter Mark Rothko as an inspirational metaphor for how they might draw their company essence or DNA. After this exercise, the team rebranded itself 'Cool Blue River' and within a year or so was one of the most profitable teams in the company. The department head transformed the offer by saying, 'When we visit clients, we are not selling flavours or fragrances but essences – creative ideas in our clients' contexts.' Part of that offer included helping clients shift their creativity and reveal their brands in a new light. Quest was a 100-year-old company, and one could easily assume it knew its purpose or reason for being. But using art and metaphor, looking at themselves through the lens or identity of Rothko, helped the oral care division to expand their vision of what they were about rather than rest complacently on their laurels.

Much of how we have observed art in business in this chapter is in relation to rediscovering play and curiosity that is every child's normal state. The rediscovery of that state reveals a new openness to change because it's an adventure rather than a trial. If leaders and bellwethers embrace this openness, then their organizations too increase their capability for transformation, innovation and inspiration. In his poem *Little Gidding*, T S Eliot mused, 'The end of all our exploring will be to arrive where we started and know the place for the first time.'[8] The last time in human history that the worlds of art and commerce naturally intertwined regularly and synergistically was in the Renaissance, that revolutionary time of human invention. Today, leaders' ability to spark success will be correlated to their willingness to rediscover lost aspects of their nature, as if from under an old and beloved rock in the garden, and remember their proficiency as creative prodigies.

One thing you can do on Monday morning

Drawing and painting are powerful enablers to unlock either what is unconscious or what we are unwilling or unable to share verbally. In strategic sessions where a team is planning their future, particularly larger themes involving mission, value proposition, trends and forces at play, the emotional state of the company, current and future customers, the leader could begin by facilitating a drawing session in order to unearth deeper thoughts and emotions. This exercise could produce a richer and more honest conversation to follow. Of course, there is enormous value not only in viewing what people draw but in asking them afterwards, 'Why did you draw that?' In explaining their picture, the individual can then express their feelings and ideas that previously only dwelled under the surface.

A more challenging but potentially more rewarding exercise is to ask a team collectively to draw the future of the group, company, industry or market on one enormous sheet of paper. In this manner, colleagues must communicate dynamically with one another, constantly check in and sense check, collaborate with one person or cluster and then another, 'yes, and...' people's ideas, and simultaneously communicate thoughts and emotions on the page. The leader should be fairly hands-off except to remind people not to overthink what they draw or to be critical of their or their teammates' outputs. If anyone is stuck and not creating something, ask them just to start drawing anything, even if they have no idea what might emerge. They could even simply add colours or textures to an image that someone else has sketched. Responding to someone else's contribution in the drawing is as valuable as inserting a brand new element. Inevitably, the vision and themes that manifest in a drawing of this communal nature are more ambitious than those the team would have envisioned merely in a conversation.

The facilitator of this collective drawing exercise can also conduct scenario planning in a similar manner. First, ask the group on one sheet of paper to draw their vision of the future together in whatever context of 'the future' is relevant. Then, put another sheet of paper alongside or perpendicular to the first and ask the group to draw another possibility based on a new input. For example, let's say the team is drawing their company's future ten years from today. After a short discussion of this work, the leader could put down a new sheet of paper that branches off from the part that illustrates their future customers and say, 'Now draw our customers of the future in a world where people feel disengaged from social media.' This is a valuable means to capture a collective view of different scenarios that can be faster than dialogue would yield and would certainly not get bogged down in disagreement, as the group simply has to keep drawing. If people disagree, then they each draw those different visions and no one is curtailed unnecessarily.

Endnotes

1 Media Education Center, 'Using images effectively in media', Williams College, February 2010, https://oit.williams.edu/files/2010/02/using-images-effectively.pdf (archived at https://perma.cc/8VGB-HHZR)

2 Interview with Giles Ford, 2020.

3 Interview with Roger Minton, 2020.

4 Interview with Peter Moolan-Feroze, 2020.

5 Chris Griffiths with Melina Costi, *Grasp the Solution* (Delhi: Proactive Press, 2011), 22.

6 Interview with Carol Robert, 6 June 2022.

7 My personal observation as the programme director of Beyond Borders.

8 T S Eliot, *Little Gidding* (London: Faber and Faber, 1942).

09
Lighting the fire

Leading creativity

L eadership is due a revolution. As I hope I have demonstrated throughout this book, we need to inject more humanity into our organizational lives. After all, companies are only going to change to the extent that their leaders are personally willing to change. This is challenging because senior executives have spent a lifetime learning to succeed in a certain way, in many cases emulating the leaders above them. If corporate life requires a different style and direction from our leaders today, that could certainly be perceived as risky or even threatening. But we also know that customers and colleagues crave and expect their leaders to be more human at work. In addition to practising new personal habits and ways of leading innovation and adaptability, becoming a creative leader must be about taking your people with you on this journey: communicating emotion, creating clarity and the right environment for a human-forward company.

When leaders suddenly change without providing context, their teams can be confused or frustrated. Practising a creative mindset is also about laying the foundations for an organization that is as human as any individual within it. Achieving this will require five steps to ensure personal and collective success:

1 Develop an inspiring personal vision.

2 Incorporate emotion into communication.

3 Attract the unusual.

4 Manage initiative lightly.

5 Be kind.

Let's take these one by one.

Develop an inspiring personal vision

At a fundamental level, this requires you to redefine for yourself what it means to manage and lead in a way that serves your team and organization rather than solely serving the history of management science. What, how and why do you do what you do, and what are the intended consequences? OK, you're changing your leadership mindset and manner? To what end? These are questions that most managers have never asked themselves even after years of doing the job. We've explored how creating a storyline will assist in informing your creative choices from television writer and producer Andrew Reich. Clarity is helpful and comforting not only for the leader but for their people. Change often fails because the vision and tactics aren't specific enough.

Incorporate emotion into communication

The late US poet laureate Maya Angelou wrote, 'I've learned that people will forget what you said, people will forget what you did, but people will never forget how you made them feel.'[1] Emotion is key to making messages stick. If you truly want your team to understand and practise creativity as a new normal, make sure they see how much that means to you, not only rationally but emotionally. We have already seen how emotion can be used to help people reconsider their capacity for change, from Alex Steele and his jazz workshops to Peter Moolan-Feroze and his art sessions for executives. You may have heard the maxim by Canadian neurologist Donald Calne that reason leads to conclusions while emotion leads to actions. Well, research has demonstrated that this hypothesis is true and not only a nice-sounding meme on social media.[2] The funny thing is that once you have made the message emotional in how you deliver it to your people, you will automatically have made your *own* commitment infinitely greater.

Attract the unusual

It is human bias to cluster with those who are like us. This is primarily because to do so feels comfortable and safe. It is not, however, a recipe for innovation. If there is one truth on which all organizational behaviour literature agrees, it is that creativity increases with diversity and decreases with sameness.[3] That's why diversity has to be more than a passive tolerance for differences. It must become an active search for the idiosyncratic, odd, peculiar and colourful.

Every time you get to hire someone, you have a wonderful opportunity to find a new perspective to challenge your mindset and that of your team. Embrace that opportunity. Understandably, you will seek certain competencies or proficiencies when hiring for a specific role, but don't look for a 'company person'. We've heard from artist Giles Ford entreating us to embrace the peculiar in order to nurture collective imagination. Find the rebel, the oddball, the piece that doesn't quite fit. It is then your challenge and gift to make sure your team accepts rather than rejects the 'otherness' of their new colleague.

During his time as chairman of Pixar, the world's most successful animated film studio, the late Steve Jobs regularly hired irregular people. One of these was Brad Bird, a former Disney animator famous for getting 'The Simpsons' off the ground. When he was approached to join Pixar, Jobs told Bird, 'The only thing we're afraid of is getting complacent. We need to bring in outside people so we keep throwing ourselves off balance.' Encouraged by Pixar's appetite for the non-conforming, Bird signed on. Soon afterwards, he explained the logic of his appointment to a journalist: 'I was brought here to cause a certain amount of disruption. I've been fired for being disruptive several times, but this is the first time I've been hired for it.'[4]

You can also retain and even enhance diversity by thinking differently about onboarding. I must admit I'm not a fan of the phrase 'onboarding' in the first place. Onboarding implies 'get on board, get with the programme, get in line', in other words, 'Conform fast!' As part of their recruitment and orientation, most companies have incredibly detailed diversity and inclusion policies, but in reality they're usually at least decent with the 'diversity' part but poor with the 'inclusion' piece. That's because you can hire for diversity; that's a policy challenge which companies, as sophisticated bureaucracies, are pretty good at. But inclusion is a cultural challenge; you see it in behaviours and habits which are much harder to change. Of course, diversity has little value if individuals aren't free to be different. Conformity neuters diversity. Despite all the rhetoric to the contrary, companies often put much more effort into training the diversity out of people through programmes that indoctrinate employees in the 'one best way' than into encouraging fresh ideas.

Too many orientation programmes focus solely on teaching new hires about the company and team they are joining and demonstrate no curiosity whatsoever about these people with all their different backgrounds, educations and life experiences. Orientation should be a lot more about them and very little about you! And keep their external perspective for as long as possible. Before the biases, lenses and preferences of the organization creep into their consciousness, do not fail to ask them at every opportunity: 'What are we doing wrong? What could we do better? What are we missing? How would you have tackled this issue or challenge in your last company? How would you compete with us? Why would you buy from us?' and so on.

Manage initiative lightly

If fostering creativity is about allowing a high degree of agency, the leader still manages the guardrails but perhaps not in the traditional way in which most organizations manage. We've heard Sir Clive Gillinson's approach at Carnegie Hall is to stay close to new team members until he's confident that their approach aligns with his expectation, and then he gives them expansive freedom. Two vanguard companies, W L Gore and Morning Star, have also made great strides to manage their people lightly, and they could not be in more traditional industries: the first is in the consumer and industrial materials industry (they make Gore-Tex, for example) and the second is in the tomato-processing industry. These organizations prompt their employees to think and act as if they own the company. There are no titles, no hierarchies, and colleagues write their own objectives. But they are held to high standards by their peers and must always demonstrate that they are improving their outcomes and impact. With a high degree of autonomy, each person becomes their personal change management department, innovation centre and entrepreneurial unit.

W L Gore is a company that is both incredibly innovative and highly disciplined. This corporation has never posted a loss in its 70-year history. How does it pull off this trick? One of the keys to Gore's innovation performance is the great amount of freedom that people have in choosing what they work on and with whom. This freedom, however, comes with strong accountability to one's peers. As a Gore associate, performance and compensation are not determined by a single boss but by several colleagues who clearly know what you've done and how you've interacted with others on a daily basis. This approach ensures that autonomy is used wisely, for example asking yourself, 'How does my idea turn an either/or tradeoff into a both/and?'

If someone at Morning Star feels that they're not contributing enough value, they can change their role or even move to another team. There's not much chance for serendipitous, creative interactions if reporting relationships and job definitions force people to work with the same small cluster of colleagues for months or years at a time. These types of companies prove that it is not work itself that strips initiative and inspiration but the way in which the majority of corporations engineer how that work is organized.

Be kind

My final entreaty is also the most personal and dear to me. My mother taught me many things, but above all she reminded me to be kind. I honestly am not convinced that there is a higher human virtue. We know the world lacks human kindness and there would never be a world where we would have 'too much'. At some point, though, the practice of management drove a schism between kindness and leadership. Sure, you sometimes have to encourage and incentivize performance, but you can always do so with empathy and kindness.

Recall that if you as a leader are personally willing to change to make creativity, adaptability, innovation and inspiration part of how you show up every day, and you are excited about encouraging the same from your team, you will still encounter fear because you're messaging and role modelling what is yet unknown or uncomfortable. Your team doesn't yet know if it will be risky for them to embark upon a new path. Your kindness and understanding, acknowledging that it's new for everyone, that we will all stumble sometimes and learn together, broadcasts the strongest signal that they will be encouraged and even rewarded to take different steps.

As I emphasized in my earlier point about emotion, the great reward you give *yourself* when you practise kindness to others is that you are more generous, forgiving, optimistic and patient with your own new journey. Don't let an expectation of perfection get in the way of progress. We simply have to start, start now and start boldly. If we are at the dawn of a new Renaissance, let me again refer to our own Renaissance artist, Mr Shakespeare, in *Hamlet*. In his masterpiece, Shakespeare knew and lamented that most human of ailments, the knowing–doing gap. *Hamlet* is still the most popular play in the English language because Hamlet's tragedy is our own all-too-familiar one – we know what we should do but we do not act. Hamlet dithers through four hours of drama. We are in turn exasperated and engrossed in his dithering. He raises dithering to its own art form. Hamlet is victim to the most recognizable plague in our human character.

Many people might watch *Hamlet* just to see how the lead actor performs the famous 'To be or not to be' soliloquy. The audience sits up a little straighter and listens a little harder when the actor laments, whispers or declaims those legendary six words. However, I don't believe that first line is the best part of the monologue. The most interesting part occurs at the end of the speech when Hamlet essentially delivers the executive summary of the entire play:

> And thus the native hue of resolution
> Is sicklied o'er with the pale cast of thought,
> And enterprises of great pith and moment
> With this regard their currents turn awry
> And lose the name of action.[5]

In other words:

> We might think that we're committed
> But then we overthink it
> And even though our plans are ambitious and inspiring
> We're distracted
> And end up doing nothing.

Creativity is not secondary, it is core to human existence, and our world of business must be included in that existence. I feel dismay when I see the creative and liberal arts diminished or dismantled by schools. As an undergraduate English major, I was astounded to read recently that some universities are even killing off their literature departments with the argument that their students won't be able to earn a living. How much of the professional services, experience and creative economies (all so critical to the prosperity of Britain, the US and many other countries) are predicated on their people's ability to analyse and communicate with precision, power and passion? How can we possibly predict in the first place what skills and inspirations people will build upon to enrich their wellbeing or prosperity? After all, Steve Jobs credited his university course in calligraphy of all things as fundamental to his combining the worlds of creativity and technology so successfully at Apple.

In a modern world where technology is almost always king, we should be careful not to let technology replace humanity. Technology is the master of scale, but it need not be our master. Technology can help us arrive at extraordinary places, but we still need to figure out what to do once we get there. Efficiency does not replace innovation, adaptability or inspiration. We're all so desperate to make our companies 'mature' places that we immunize them from those very qualities that we need now more than ever. Remember the experiment from Professor George Land which demonstrated how the creative genius we all possess as children slowly withers and dies. Yet we know and acknowledge that we desperately need that creativity in corporate life. We recognize what it looks and feels like. Remember childhood: 'Think of it. Heightened sensitivity, idealism, honesty, a sense of wonder and curiosity, a simple and loving heart, and yet we all can't wait to be rational adults.'[6] It is up to people, not technology, to create purpose, invent, adapt, engage, connect. In that regard, disciplines like art should not be seen as a fun diversion but as the source of crucial insights and skills. A creative, humanistic mindset isn't a luxury, it is your competitive advantage.

Endnotes

1 Carmine Gallo, 'The Maya Angelou quote that will radically improve your business', *Forbes*, 31 May 2014, https://www.forbes.com/sites/carminegallo/2014/05/31/the-maya-angelou-quote-that-will-radically-improve-your-business/ (archived at https://perma.cc/P2QB-RQW7)

2 Chip Heath and Dan Heath, *Made to Stick* (New York: Random House, 2007).

3 With thanks to my late mentor Gareth Jones for emphasizing this point.

4 Kevin Coupe, 'What Planet Pixar can teach retailers', Morning Newsbeat, 3 August 2004, https://morningnewsbeat.com/2004/08/03/what-planet-pixar-can-teach-retailers/ (archived at https://perma.cc/9QJ5-HAT6)

5 William Shakespeare, *Hamlet*, in *The Riverside Shakespeare*, ed. G Blakemore Evans (Boston: Houghton Mifflin, 1974), III, i, 83–87.

6 Arthur Gogatz and Reuben Mondejar, *Business Creativity: Breaking the Invisible Barriers* (Houndmills: Palgrave Macmillan, 2005).

ACKNOWLEDGEMENTS

I have a secret editor, the only one I allow to see my unfiltered scribbles, psychobabbles, laments and hyperboles because she is much more learned in the craft of writing than I and is pure in her goal to improve the work, and that is my wife, Elizabeth. Many have contributed to this book, but she read those first drafts in their loopiest states. As I write this, I think then that I not only have to thank her again but apologize that she had to wade through quite a lot of dust to identify the gold. I am a lucky man.

Many thanks to everyone who agreed to be interviewed for this book. This study would not have been possible without your stories.

Thank you to my wonderful and supportive editor, Matt James. We talked about the possibility of working on this project together way back in 2019 while chatting at a book launch. He was unfailingly reliable at keeping in touch as I refined the proposal. I understand that *Sparking Success* is his first commission with Kogan Page and I am honoured to be his inaugural collaboration. Long may it continue.

I am beyond grateful to the entire Kogan Page team for believing in this book from the beginning, including Martin Skerrett, Viv Church, Arthur Thompson, Heather Langridge, Zexna Opara and Helen Kogan, Jaini Haria and Shannon Branch in sales and marketing and Amy Joyner in rights and licensing.

Many thanks to Christopher Newson, Nick Wallwork and J L Stermer for their commercial advice.

I unreservedly thank the English departments of Bellarmine College Preparatory in San Jose, California and Yale University for nurturing my love of language and writing.

Cliché though it may sound, I could not have achieved anything without the support and love of my family and to a person you have been exceptional in my life. May I add special thanks and love to my dear dad and the beautiful memory of my mom. I was a lucky boy.

INDEX

Page numbers in *italic* indicate figures or tables

CPSIA information can be obtained
at www.ICGtesting.com
Printed in the USA
LVHW071308170723
751165LV00009B/51